WHY WE WRITE

WHY WE WRITE

PERSONAL STATEMENTS AND PHOTOGRAPHIC PORTRAITS OF 25 TOP **SCREENWRITERS**

EDITED AND PHOTOGRAPHED BY LORIAN TAMARA ELBERT

SILMAN-JAMES PRESS   LOS ANGELES

First Edition
10 9 8 7 6 5 4 3 2 1

Library of Congress Cataloging-in-Publication Data

Why we write : personal statements and photographic portraits of
25 top screenwriters / edited and photographed by Lorian Tamara Elbert.
— 1st ed.
p. cm.
1. Motion picture authorship. 2. Screenwriters—United States—Interviews.
3. Screenwriters—United States—Portraits.
I. Elbert, Lorian Tamara, 1966-
PN1996.W395 1999   808.2'3—dc21   98-48736

ISBN: 1-879505-45-2

Prints of the photographs in this book are available from Lorian Tamara Elbert.
For information call (323) 856-6282 or email photo@jps.net

Cover design by Wade Lageose, Art Hotel

Printed and bound in the United States of America

Silman-James Press
1181 Angelo Drive
Beverly Hills, CA 90210

For the Abramowitz family, my true friends,
and in memory of my Godmother, Louise Stallard.

CONTENTS

FOREWORD
by Kenneth Turan

Words and pictures. Pictures and words.

Here is a collection of the faces we almost never see. Few people are as essential to a film's success as its screenwriters, and few are as invisible. It's not an accident.

Everyone in the movie business wants to be considered creative. Even if they got to be powerful industry players by being adroit gameplayers and back-stabbers, creative is how they now want to be known. But if these people are going to be creative, it has to be at the expense of the true and original creators, the writers, the people without whose ideas none of this would be possible.

So writers are rewritten. Browbeaten, minimalized, ignored, battered by unfortunate ideas from unlikely sources. These suggestions can at times be helpful, for film is a collaborative art after all. But as one friend with several screen credits put it, "I can be miserable or I can direct. I've decided to be miserable."

Look at the following pictures of writers at their ease. They don't, by and large, exude the glamour of often-photographed stars, nor do they, with a few exceptions, have the confident, powerful look that's visible in shots of directors. There is a word for the way these writers mostly look, and it's "worried." What can go wrong? Everything. And it often does. But they keep at it, and it's a good thing. For without them, there wouldn't be any movies worth seeing. None at all.

ACKNOWLEDGMENTS

Thank you to all the screenwriters who made this book a reality through their encouragement and wisdom. Meeting such incredible individuals was a wonderful experience.

Thanks to everyone who has contributed in some way to making this book a reality, especially Marci and William and Jennifer Landis, Steven Smith, Betty Woo, Scott Roeben, Leah Cavell, Andrea Hecker, Lilly Abramowitz, Sam Guttman, John Maxwell, Marty Shapiro, Shooting Star Agency, Bill Bruns, Roberts R. Donohue, Edward Maupin, Bill Ridgeway, Habbat of Brentwood, Habbat of Westwood, California Jewish Center, St. Monica's Catholic Church, Hirsch Perlman, Greg Dahl, John Cotter, Michael Ferris, Winston Grace, Richard Walter, Ann Gray, and Kenneth Turan.

I especially want to thank Gwen and Jim at Silman-James Press for believing in me and for publishing this book. And to all the wonderful people in my life who have been and continue to be positive, supportive, and encouraging.

INTRODUCTION

Screenwriters write because they cherish the adventure of telling their stories. And in Hollywood, screenwriting is always an adventure.

Most screenwriters learn to survive, and even enjoy, the various types of roller-coaster rides required to succeed in Hollywood. The rides may sometimes make them nauseous, but, eventually, these writers throw their arms in the air and scream or laugh as they enjoy the twists and turns and ups and downs.

I personally despise roller coasters. I'm afraid that gravity will cease for a split second—just long enough for my car to fly straight off into the air. My fear, which is morbid for me, is enjoyable for others. Many screenwriters relish the thrill of being scared out of their wits by stress, pressure, and the premonition that it all may end very soon. They learn to thrive on looming deadlines and unexpected changes and survive both the Hell and Heaven of telling another story.

Screenwriters manage to work on simultaneous projects, write and direct, and balance family life and work. Most are intensely self-motivated and prolific. Their obsessive need to tell stories that millions of people will share, coupled with the demands of spouses, children, agents, managers, publicists, and mortgages, provide them with ample incentives to write their next screenplays. Yet, only five percent of the approximately 8,500 Writers Guild members actually make a living from their writing.

Most of the writers in this book have been storytellers in one form or another since their childhoods. Some recognized their own knack for it, others were encouraged by friends and family. All were powerfully affected by their early moviegoing experiences. Watching films led to the self-realization that they were born with keen and amazingly verbal and visual memories that they could translate from their minds to the minds of others.

Brilliant screenwriters have the talent to communicate in the language of film. Their genius lies in their ability to write down, page after page, powerful emotions and visual images that can make audiences feel, see, and hear a story that takes them to another world. They have something to say that keeps people lining up at the box office to be informed, entertained, and sometimes transformed. These screenwriters are inspired by their peers, their friends, their children, and all of the world around them. They can't just sit back and watch, they are driven to comment on their experiences and share these comments with countless other souls.

To succeed, they find ways to deal with pain, disappointment, rejection, critics, and executives. Knowing full well that all of what they write will not always end up on the screen, they learn how to collaborate with, help, and respect the directors of their films. They learn what works and master their craft. But they also push themselves and never take the process for granted.

Many screenwriters acknowledge that most moviegoers (and some film industry executives) do not understand and respect the writer's contribution to a film. If the general public understood that screenwriters face 120 blank pages that they turn into 120 pages filled with characters, scenes, descriptions, actions, and dialogue, they might cease believing that actors make up their lines and that the director is a film's sole author. To this end, screenwriters simply ask that their work be properly and consistently credited in magazines, newspapers, video guides, and throughout the media that regularly acknowledges the work of actors and directors.

Screenwriters are as integral a part of the filmmaking process as the film emulsion is to the images we see on the screen. They need and deserve understanding, appreciation, and respect. They are critical of themselves and the world, sometimes even cynical, but most still yearn for happy beginnings and happy endings.

• • • • •

The photography

I shot all the photographs for this book in available light, mostly at the writers' Los Angeles-area homes. One writer was photographed in a Santa Barbara garden, and three writers flew to Los Angeles and were photographed wherever we could get together—a hotel room, an office, and at LAX.

I utilized a Nikon FM2 camera with Nikon lenses, Illford film, and Illford paper. I hand-printed and toned all the photographs myself.

PORTRAITS
AND
STATEMENTS

RANDALL WALLACE

SCREENPLAYS

Braveheart (1995)

The Man in the Iron Mask (1998)

I love to tell stories. Here is one.

My grandfather was a farmer in Tennessee. During the Depression he had to go into town to find work, and being a big man—six feet three, and over 200 pounds of muscle—he soon found a job doing manual labor at an ice-making plant. On his first day, the foreman came up to him and gave him this welcome: "Do what I tell ya and we'll get on okay. But I just want you to know that we got lots of niggers that work on this crew, and I got to cuss at 'em to make 'em work, so if I ever call you a son-of-a-bitch don't pay me no mind, I don't mean nothin' by it, that's just the way I am."

And my grandfather, who was a Baptist deacon with a number of colored friends, looked down at the foreman and said, "I understand. And I just want you to know that if you call me a son-of-a-bitch, and I hit you in the face with a claw hammer, don't pay me no mind, I don't mean nothin' by it, that's just the way I am."

I never met my grandfather; he died the year before I was born. And yet I know him—through his children, of course, and through my grandmother, who loved him through her last breath. But perhaps I know him most vividly and fully because of that story which tells me who he was, and how he was.

That's what stories do. They aren't philosophy or history lessons or sermons or propaganda; though they may contain all those elements, they are greater than them all. The Bible itself is a collection of narratives of the devilish and the divine, of the fallen and the redeemed.

We all have our codes, and we all fail to completely live up to them. We all have our theologies, and they are intellectual abstractions.

But good stories have emotion and passion, they have bite and bone. They embrace our shortcomings and point out our potential. And they are living things. Some stories have been told unchanged for thousands of years; others pick up something from the teller each time they are told.

I hope I will tell stories that will matter to my children. I believe, if I do, that my grandfather will smile down on me, from the Heaven where he surely is.

LAWRENCE KONNER

SCREENPLAYS

The Jewel of the Nile (1985), w/Mark Rosenthal

Superman IV: The Quest for Peace (1987), w/Mark Rosenthal

The In Crowd (1988), w/Mark Rosenthal

Desperate Hours (1990), w/Mark Rosenthal and Joseph Hayes

Star Trek VI: The Undiscovered Country (1991), w/Mark Rosenthal and Leonard Nimoy

For Love or Money (1993), w/Mark Rosenthal

The Beverly Hillbillies (1993), w/Mark Rosenthal

Mighty Joe Young (1998), w/Mark Rosenthal

Mercury Rising (1998), w/Mark Rosenthal

Most screenwriters like watching movies more than I do. For me, it's never an unalloyed pleasure. If the movie is any good—and sometimes, even when it isn't—my desire to have been part of the making of it overwhelms any possibility of simply enjoying the thing.

This was the case even when I was a kid. My friends and I went every Saturday afternoon to the same theater. We went regardless of what was showing, even if it meant seeing *Demetrius and the Gladiators* for the eighth week running. While the boys around me lost themselves in cop and cowboy fantasies (gladiators were harder to fantasize about— they wore skirts), I was resentful. I wanted to be part of the show, not part of the audience. I suspected even then that it was better to be working at the carnival than to be one of the rubes lining up to get in.

Screenwriting is a business tough enough to steamroll any child's aspirations into pavement. Samuel Goldwyn once famously called screenwriters "schmucks with Underwoods," and many producers and directors continue to think of us as not much more than schmucks with laptops. Many of us are, to be sure, well-paid schmucks, but most of us feel our contribution is undervalued and misunderstood.

Despite this, it turns out that I was right to want in. There is a power attached to screenwriting—a power I discovered in the first weeks of my first paying job as a staff writer on a television drama. The producer called late one night: a new scene needed to be written for the next day's shooting. I had the not particularly original idea of setting it during a rainstorm. I began by typing the words . . . EXT. SMITH HOUSE - DAY - RAIN. The studio messenger picked up the pages at three A.M.; I slept for several hours, then drove to the set. The crew was deep into preparations to make the weather I had ordered. Rain machines had been brought in, streets were being washed down. Burberries were being tailored to fit the players. Thousands of dollars were being spent, hundreds of man-hours expended. My megalomania had been aroused. I thought; Perhaps next time, I'll type - SNOW.

The poet said, "Only God can make a tree." The poet lied. A screenwriter can also make a tree. Or a forest fire to consume that tree. Or the brave man to put out that fire. A screenwriter can make a herd of buffalo, or cause the city of Buffalo to be invaded by giant tarantulas. A screenwriter can make any team he wants win the World Series. And on a good day, a lucky day, he can write a moment of human truth that makes someone in the darkened movie theater sit up and say, "Yes! That's just how it is!"

SCOTT ALEXANDER

SCREENPLAYS

Problem Child (1990), w/Larry Karaszewski

Problem Child 2 (1991), w/Larry Karaszewski

Ed Wood (1994), w/Larry Karaszewski

The People vs. Larry Flynt (1996), w/Larry Karaszewski

That Darn Cat (1997), w/Larry Karaszewski

Why do I write? I write to express my feelings about the bizarre world we live in. I worry that society, politics, and culture long ago turned into a dull pap, and I've always felt driven to comment upon it, in my own off-center way.

I fell into the world of movies while still in elementary school. A love of the Marx Brothers led to early experiments in Super-8, doing animation. However, I quickly discovered I didn't have the patience for filmmaking one frame at a time. So in junior high, I graduated to live-action epics, shooting one-weekend wonders with my eager friends. As I look back on these films, I realize that my recurring themes for life were already set in stone: DON'T BUY THAT CRAP! DON'T TRUST THAT LEADER! DON'T SETTLE FOR MIDDLE-OF-THE-ROAD LAMENESS! Even at the age of fourteen, I was restless and critical of the pandering mediocrity I suspected was everywhere. I was already satirizing the junk that we all settle for. Authority figures were idiots. Consumer products were worthless. Characters were beaten into accepting jobs and lives they didn't particularly want. The lone figures who spoke out usually got destroyed or blown-up.

And then I got to high school.

Actually, that joke doesn't particularly go anywhere. My stories simply grew *more* obsessive. My crowning teenage achievement was a thirty-minute Super-8 epic called *Myron*. In this story, a pathetic little guy spends his life getting the crap kicked out of him. One day he finally decides to speak up . . . which only leads to humiliation, mockery, and the man literally evaporating.

The lesson? Don't even *try* to fix things.

In college, my dorm roommate was Larry Karaszewski. Senior year, we decided to write a feature script. My old paranoid themes were still there: THEY'RE GONNA RIP YOU OFF! THEY'RE ALL CROOKS! But now, working with Larry, something changed—in addition to the usual browbeaten protagonist, there was a new character . . . the anarchist. In this script, his name was Kermit, an absurdly confident, totally incompetent cat burglar. Looking back now, Kermit represented our future. He was an outsider. He was loud. He was pure id. He was funny. He was frowned upon by most of the characters . . . but he didn't care.

Since then, practically all of our scripts have had a version of Kermit, the unstable loon who slams up against society's rules and speaks out.

The Problem Child was a shameless example. Ed Wood was a screw-up, but oblivious. Larry Flynt brought a rage we had never tried. Our newest, Andy Kaufman, is pure dissonance, a man who's literally his own enemy.

These scripts have brought me immense pleasure, giving a ranting voice to someone who's otherwise quite repressed. My real life is totally inhibited: A clichéd domestic existence, happily playing in my yard with my wife and kids. But through the scripts, I'm able to act out and scream at everything that bugs me. The loudmouths vent on my behalf. Obviously, I'm not the first to try this—millions of satirists do it daily. How Larry and I attempt to be original is through our odd tone—a layering of sweetness over insidiousness. We toss in obtuse buffoons, frantic straight men, and opinionated blowhards. And then, we put the point of view smack inside our madman's head, so that the audience can empathize and understand.

In closing, I shouldn't leave the impression that I'm some kind of bitter curmudgeon. Our movies *always* have hopeful endings. The character may be flawed, but he usually triumphs in some cockeyed way and beats the system. Ed Wood gets fame. Andy Kaufman cheats death. They find redemption . . . and just maybe bring some positive change to the world. It's not all dour. Perhaps I even have an affinity with one of my role models, Billy Wilder: I'm just an optimist disguised as a cynic.

TOM SCHULMAN

SCREENPLAYS

Dead Poets Society (1989)

Honey, I Shrunk the Kids (1989), w/Ed Naha

What About Bob? (1991)

Medicine Man (1992), w/Sally Robinson

8 Heads in a Duffel Bag (1997)

Holy Man (1998)

If you think writers create from nothing or that writing is a lonely occupation, you are wrong. Writers create from life, and writers are never lonely. Whenever I get writer's stasis (never *ever* use the "b" word), I put on a comfortable pair of shoes and take off walking. Even on a dreary day, when there isn't a soul in sight, life explodes all around me.

Alongside Ocean Avenue in Santa Monica, there is a thin strip of grassy park atop the crumbling palisades that overlook the beaches of the Pacific. Many of the park benches are marked by plaques, most of them memorials. "Our beloved Bill, we will never forget you," reads one. "For our dearest Jessie, 1948 to 1992," reads another. "In memory of our friend Sarah," reads still another. You can't help but wonder who these people were and how they lived and died.

I pass Bill's bench frequently, and I have come to the conclusion that Bill was the victim of an insurance scam. I feel strongly that Bill was poisoned by his family, probably using Clorox, and after he died they erected this plaque to him with a great sense of irony. They will never forget Bill because his death is paying for their summer house in Aix-en-Provence.

Jessie, I feel certain, died in a car wreck. She had just broken up with her husband and was driving in a teary-eyed rage when she veered into the freeway median, flipped, and rolled under a truck. Emergency workers spent forty-five minutes using the Jaws of Life to rescue Jessie, but two days into what looked like a completely successful recovery, she slipped into a coma and died—of a broken heart. Today, Jessie's parents walk the palisades, no longer touching each other, cursing their fate, consumed by despair. Jessie's widower married a show girl and works as a dealer in Reno. Asked if he feels responsible for Jessie's death (he was, in fact, two-timing her), he said, "Life deals us losing cards all the time. Smart people move on to the next hand."

I believe that Sarah was a political activist and old-guard lefty. The friends who bought her plaque were her Communist party cellmates from the '30s. Other "friends" named her at the McCarthy hearings, and Sarah spent years in emotional and occupational exile. Sarah could be charming, but she could also be grating. She once stood up at a Yom Kippur service in Beverly Hills and accused the entire congregation of still worshipping the gold calf. She publicly accused her Catholic friends of having no concept of the meaning of forgiveness—for which they never forgave her. In memory of Sarah, the friends who bought her plaque still haven't paid for it.

The parks and streets of Santa Monica are teaming with other memories, too. Every piece of ground or cement you walk on, every "space" through which you pass, has stories to tell—perhaps thousands of stories. When you stand at the light at Third and Arizona, you know that maybe just the night before a couple stood in the same place, arguing about a movie, each asking themselves how they ever were going to find someone who really loved them. An hour later, a homeless person—who spent his youth raising a family he hasn't seen in a decade—stood wondering where to go to watch the last episode of *Seinfeld*. Two hundred years ago, on this very spot, a Chumash warrior was captured by the Spaniards and bludgeoned. Every square inch of ground in every city and hamlet on Earth practically yowls with stories of courage, brutality, joy, sadness, love, friendship, disappointment, and faith, but without someone to tell these stories, none of this and none of us will be remembered.

Think about it the next time you go for a walk. Think about it the next time you go anywhere. If you are a writer, you are never without a story to tell and never without a purpose in life. And no matter what you do for a living—as the old song says—you never walk alone.

GARY
ROSS

SCREENPLAYS

Big (1988)

Mr. Baseball (1992)

Dave (1993)

Lassie (1994), w/Elizabeth Anderson and Matthew Jacobs

Pleasantville (1998)

I've always thought that screenwriting was the most crucial part of the filmmaking process. Now that I've directed a film, I still feel that way. So often you hear the uniformed response: "The screenplay is just the blueprint for the film." But how many buildings turn out well with a bad set of blueprints? Or more importantly: Who's more crucial to the job, your architect or your contractor?

Screenwriting is a strange hybrid of many things: a craft and an art . . . a solitary act of creation and a collaborative process involving hundreds of people. In its purest form, screenwriting is as fulfilling as any act of personal expression. At the same time, a screenplay must serve as the business plan for a hundred-million-dollar investment.

No wonder writers are always complaining.

And yet, at its best, nothing is more sublime. It just takes a little getting used to. In *Seymour: An Introduction*, J.D. Salinger gives great advice about writing. He says that writing is easy. You just pick the book you want to read more than any in the world, and you write it for yourself.

Screenwriting is not much different. At the inception of a movie, the screenwriter is the MOST powerful part of the process, not the least. He is the only one who is ever in control of all the elements in the film at one time. The performances are the ones that occur in his own head. The locations are what he sees when he closes his eyes. The shadings and nuances are tailor-made to his sensibilities. There are no missing pieces of coverage. No characterizations that miss the mark. The film is "perfect" because no one has shot it yet. And perfect can be a pretty nice thing.

Obviously the filmmaking process will change all of this, but the more an original vision can remain, the more compelling the film will ultimately be. Some would argue (excessively, I feel) that the director supplies this vision in his role as the "auteur." But as an act of creation, this is an "after-market" addition—one that augments the original artistic point of view but never supplants it. And on some deep, dark level, everyone in the film business understands this. They have seen too many rudderless productions. The successful film is one with a *reason for being*, and so the writer who has done his job well and sticks to his guns REMAINS the most powerful person on the film, whether he realizes it or not.

MICHAEL FERRIS

SCREENPLAYS

Femme Fatale (1991) w/John Brancato

Into the Sun (1992) w/John Brancato

Interceptor (1993) w/John Brancato

The Net (1995) w/John Brancato

The Game (1997) w/John Brancato

Unlike those so-called "well-rounded individuals" who occasionally venture into this realm, I've been obsessed with motion pictures pretty much since childhood. At the age of thirteen or so, I indulged this fixation by rounding up socially challenged kids like myself and putting them in Super-8 mini-epics such as *Day of Destruction, The Castle of Doctor Mean,* and *The Vampire of Fairview Drive.* Years later, I majored in film, though at Harvard they called it "Visual and Environmental Studies" and focused on things like the experimental work of Stan Brackage and grainy black-and-white documentaries about stillbirth in the cattle industry. Shortly after returning to my native Los Angeles, I began writing with my college pal, John Brancato, thus beginning a partnership that has remained fruitful to this day.

John and I first collaborated on a low-budget comedy called *My Funny Valentine,* concerning the exploits of a trailer-park couple who go on a brief crime spree, during which the guy loses his arm and has it replaced by a mechanical steel prosthesis that he can play like a musical instrument. They become big MTV stars, until the law catches up with them and they're forced to hitch a ride with a marijuana smuggler into Alaska, where they flee across the Bering Strait and into the Soviet Union and end up playing coffee houses in Siberia. It didn't sell—no doubt, the studios were all developing projects just like it.

The script did get us some attention at Vestron Pictures, however, where they hired us to develop an idea of their own called *Old MacDonald's Farm*: a comedy about a farmer and his three beautiful daughters who start murdering travelling salesmen and grinding them into sausages. It did seem a little peculiar inasmuch as Vestron had already released *Motel Hell*, which was a comedy about a farmer and his wife who kill tourists and turn them into sausages, as well as *Blood Diner*, which was a comedy about a diner where they kill the customers and . . . well, you get the idea. We were learning our first lesson about Hollywood—if it feels good once, keep doing it till you go blind—and, moreover, we were finally getting paid to write together. The movie never got made, of course, and Vestron Pictures went out of business shortly thereafter, but by then John and I were off and running.

Now that we have a couple of reasonably successful movies behind us, I must admit I look back with a peculiar nostalgia on the mid-eighties, a time that my booze- and tear-stained journals affectionately describe as "the suicide years." During the day, I made the most of my Ivy League diploma, not to mention a subsistent living as an editor at *Hus-*

tler magazine, producing "girl copy" for truck drivers, prison inmates, and sweaty-minded armchair rapists everywhere. Evenings were spent with John, cranking out low-budget, late-night cable fodder for the likes of Roger Corman and Fangoria Films. Our pseudonymous output included *The Unborn*, a story about mutant killer babies; *MindWarp*, a futuristic adventure about flesh-eating underground mutants; *Watchers II*, which concerned the exploits of a boy, a dog, and a mutant; and *Flight of the Black Angel*, a fighter-pilot action thriller that, uncharacteristically, had no mutants in it whatsoever. In fact, after *Black Angel*, we somehow got typecast as fighter-pilot action thriller writers, and were employed to write two or three more, even though John and I had never been closer to the inside of an F-16 than the Macintosh flight-simulator program. Our one attempt at an "art film" during this period, *Femme Fatale*, was dismissed by the L.A. *Times* as "shallow, verbose, and uninspired," though it still crops up on late-night TV from time to time, retitled *Fatal Woman*, so people won't be confused into thinking they're seeing a Gérard Depardieu picture or something.

These are the experiences that are routinely described as "character building" and, frankly, I wouldn't have it any other way. What's the point of selling your first script for three-quarters of a million dollars or becoming an overnight sensation at Sundance? Give me character any day . . . . At any rate, when we sold our spec script, *The Game*, in the summer of '92, we figured our worries were finally at an end. Unfortunately, we sold it to MGM, while they were in the midst of their legal crises with Italian financier Giancarlo Paretti, and incapable of issuing a coherent press release, much less financing a major motion picture. A turnaround deal ensued, which placed the project at Propaganda, and plunged us into five years of what is charitably described as "development hell," during which the director was replaced, we rewrote the script a few dozen times, were fired, re-hired, and fired again. (Oddly, the final film is remarkably similar to our first draft.) Second lesson of Hollywood learned: the more they love it, the more strenuously they're going to insist you beat it to death with a stick.

During this period, we also wrote *The Net* for Irwin Winkler, a picture that wound up being finished and released prior to *The Game*. Asked to create a moody, paranoid thriller along the lines of *Three Days of the Condor* or *The Parallax View*, we saw our original, darkly ambiguous ending replaced by one in which Sandra Bullock knocks the bad guy off a catwalk with a fire extinguisher. Thus, our third and final lesson: the words "Sandra Bullock" and "darkly ambiguous" are unlikely to ever occupy the same sentence again. (Not as all-encompassing as the first two, I'll grant, but potentially valuable nonetheless.)

As of this writing, we're waiting to hear what will become of *Remote Control*, a script we sold to Imagine about a guy who discovers a device that affects the flow of time the way a VCR remote controls a videotape; it's based on a true story, of course. But since *The Net* and *The Game* both performed reasonably well, we'll no doubt be cranking out a series of paranoiac thrillers with monosyllabic titles preceded by definite articles; prepare yourself for *The Hunt, The Scare, The Fish*, etc.

This pretty much brings me up to date. Although success has clearly gone to my head, making me the sort of insufferable megalomaniac I once held in contempt, I hasten to add that there's more to my new-found lifestyle than Academy Awards parties, Dom Perignon and Prozac for breakfast, multiple call waiting, and private helicopters with built-in hot tubs and waterproof fax machines. Why, even as I dictate these words to my nude secretary/dominatrix, my mind is elsewhere, mulling over new ideas, seeking new inspiration, sucking up to the muse if you will . . . *The Bomb, The Blurb, The Mime . . . Karaoke, the Movie . . . Die Hard* in a dirigible . . . a romantic comedy set against the fast-paced world of canine blood sports . . . .

Jeez, look at the time. You can stop typing now, Ilsa, I'm ready for my punishment.

KASI LEMMONS

SCREENPLAYS

Eve's Bayou (1997)

create best in the half-dream state between consciousness and unconsciousness. In other words, writing is what I do instead of sleeping. Because I'm not fully awake, I don't have the burden of rationality. My imagination can run blissfully wild. Because I'm not fully asleep, I have control over the images. I can watch them and direct them at the same time.

In this manner I am able to compose whole sequences so that by the time I sit in front of the intimidatingly blank screen of my computer, I am basically describing and interpreting what I've already seen, weeding out the ridiculous from the inspired (though sometimes I keep a bit of ridiculousness in, just for good measure).

The downside to this process is that I'm often tired, clumsy, and fuzzy-minded while others are crisp and well-rested, able to make snap decisions and engage in stinging repartee. The upside is that even during the day I'm sleepwalking, neither entirely present nor entirely removed, in a half-dream state that allows me to do more imagining, to add to and embellish what I wrote down from the night before. I think day-dreaming insomniacs make good writers, though maybe not good presidents or operators of heavy machinery.

When I'm not writing, I'm much more on the ball, more focused, much quicker to respond to the punchline of a joke. It might be helpful for writers with my particular idiosyncrasies to have an additional occupation that requires them to be on their toes, to wake up and smell the proverbial coffee, so as to not be permanently mired in the netherworld of imagination.

For me, writing and directing is the perfect combination. I find directing to be an invigorating experience, like jumping into icy water, or jumping off a cliff. There are thousands of decisions to make, hundreds of names to remember, and working hours that can render even the most die-hard insomniac exhausted.

I find writing warm, fuzzy, lonely, and pleasant. I sense the outside world impressionistically, as if from the womb. I find directing fast, furious, vivid, and terrifying. Like the shock of birth after the comfort of incubation.

A girl could find balance in a life like this. Or try to.

PEN
DENSHAM

SCREENPLAYS

The Zoo Gang (1985), w/John Watson, co-directed

Robin Hood: Prince of Theives (1991), w/John Watson

A Gnome Named Norm (1992)

Moll Flanders (1996), directed

WHY WE WATCH MOVIES

Some ruminations on having a monkey for an uncle.

As a very amateur anthropologist, I am always awed by the unique human phenomena of an audience falling into a trance while watching a film. Frequently, I try to catch a glance of my fellows in that darkened theater. Strangely tranquil, yet unconsciously moving their faces to mimic the expressions of the actors on the screen . . . A "good" movie keeps us woven in its dream. We never stop to ask, "Where did that orchestra come from?" We never flinch when a character jumps forward from a wide shot to a close-up. We do not ask where the characters go when they step out of frame. We do not even question incredible time jumps and contradictory cuts between images. Only in a "bad" movie do we wake up and look at our watches.

When a movie works, it is a weird and wondrous hypnotic rapture.

Researchers say a child watching a television actually uses less calories than a youngster lying in a bed. They also say that a baby mimics its mother's mouth movements from the day it is born. To me that means, right from birth, we engage in the act of being entertained . . . and something very mysterious is happening.

We seem to be willing to pay good money and put up with a high degree of discomfort, from hiring the babysitter, traveling to and fro, lining up in all kinds of weather, etc. . . . when we anticipate a good voyage into that blissful state of being "an audience." I do not think it is an accident that we find these experiences fulfilling. For my exploratory purpose I've coined the term the "Learning Trance" to try and define why our species loves the Movies, Theater, Storytelling . . . From my unscientific extrapolations of the theories of Evolutionary Psychology, I have come to believe that the desire to be in a Learning Trance watching a dramatic experience unfold and resolve is biologically programmed into us because it must have been amazingly useful.

Extraordinarily, we and the Chimpanzee both share almost 98 percent of the same genes. We're more closely related than the Chimp is to its next closest kin, the Gorilla! And despite our living in a highly technological world, in many ways we still act like a Primate that inherited its mating rituals, hierarchical society, and even the love for its young, because they were successful natural adaptations.

An Eye to the Future.

I believe by intensely observing the successes and failures of others, our ape ancestors gained vital knowledge that they could employ to change their own behavior, heighten their chances to survive, and protect their young. By intently observing how Uncle Chimp got cornered and eaten by a lion, or why he dropped dead after eating the wrong berries or failed when he fought the Alpha male for first rights on the band's eligible females, the ability to concentrate and learn from observation was a powerfully self-selecting skill for survival. It even explains why we slow down to observe traffic accidents. The instinct to learn from another's tragedy is a safety trait bred in through millennia . . . and the complacent ape who ignored the opportunity to observe and learn . . . drove too fast round the next bend and crashed on the road to the Ice Age.

Lend me your ears.

When *homo habilus* included the development of speech and oral history in his mental toolbox, man became one of the very few beasts whose elders lived beyond the age of reproduction. Why? Because the information and wisdom carried in those older brains led to the survival of those closest to them. The grandfather could protect his gene investment by sticking around long enough to guide his offspring verbally as well as physically to the only water hole available during that rare period of drought. Those who could retain information and tales that helped protect and bind the group together gained a genetic immortality. Holding an audience and the art of listening intently to oral history became as useful as observing. (Although quite where Stand-up Comedy comes in confounds me!)

So what the h..l does this have to do with movies?

When watching a movie, I sometimes try and analyze my trance state of being an audience. Up in my brain front, I seem to love watching the actors simulating their emotions and tracking the story but, in the back of my head, I can catch myself making mental notes about my own responses to these situations. Would I go into that room on *Halloween*? Would I kiss Sharon Stone? Would I fight Darth Vader? Internal calculations that are akin to mental rehearsals for possible life events. Useful stuff. I do not actually have to die to figure out how to keep Brutus and his fellow Senators from ganging up on me. It's entirely possible that the act of falling into a Learning Trance simulates the state of dreaming, that extraordinary fourth dimension of the brain's processes.

There's also a dangerous side to the Learning Trance as we are easily manipulated when we are in this state. It is called "advertising" or "propaganda" and it works almost too well. Hypnotized, we are vulnerable to suggestion and often can end up mimicking the actors buying "that" car, "that" lipstick, "those" cigarettes, "that" politician. Believe me, if the ability to manipulate the human animal in a Learning Trance didn't work, corporations wouldn't spend tens of billions of dollars annually to con us into unconsciously buying their products.

From Sophocles to Eszterhas.

Joseph Campbell's studies of myths, legends, and religions suggested that exactly the same story components cropped up in every culture, language, and historical age. Therefore, the human animal seems to like seeing the same stories over and over again, with only slight variations of time, place, or character. (Ergo, television.)

If you turn around the theory (that all cultures tell the same stories), I believe it proves that all stories are basically from exactly the same root . . . the most primary needs and experiences of the human animal. That may be why we say there are only five or six major plots. In a very oversimplified way, I interpret this to mean that all stories come from the fundamental issues of human biology.

They are about how to find a mate . . . Love stories.

How to find food and survive . . . Disaster and treasure-hunting tales.

How to avoid being hunted and killed . . . Murder mysteries and Creature films—from *Jaws* to *Jurassic Park*.

Male-conflict stories . . . Where two bull-humans bash at each other and the winner mates happily ever after with the Alpha female. *High Noon*, *Rocky*, *Face/Off*, etc.

Why are we happy when Cinderella marries the Prince? Is it because she has managed to engage a mate whose royal status will give her young a better chance to survive? What do *Robin Hood, Snow White and the Seven Dwarfs, Star Wars, The Dirty Dozen*, and *The Seven Samurai* have in common? Are they basic folk plots that encourage an altruistic group-heroism that defends others that we recognize as being like us, so that "our" tribe can have the opportunity to survive and reproduce?

Why does Shakespeare last through generations? Because his core interest is about the same basic elements of human nature that are powerfully important to survival and success, no matter what period of human history one lives in? The mystery of staring into a skull's eye sockets and wondering what happened to "Poor Yorick" is as unknowable now as it has been for all time. Fashions, cultures, nations, religions come and go . . . our biology does not change so quickly. Kings, Bosses, Bullies, Heroes, and Alpha apes still rise and fall, leading to everyone's pecking order being changed.

Ah . . . but, we're just trying to entertain people!

Yes, but it's also possible that we Writers and Filmmakers are modern Shaman inheriting a long and respectful history, the art of interpreting human nature and the mysteries of our existence.

As technology delivers vast global audiences to interact with our creations seven days a week, around the clock, around the globe . . . For the first time in history we have the opportunity to weave compassionate human dramas that simultaneously reach out to all the nations of this Earth . . . We may be responsible for finally helping EVOLVE *homo sapiens* to viewing ourselves as one single global tribe . . . .

. . . Humankind. Hopefully with the emphasis on "kind."

Evolutionary Psychology, or "Psycho-Biology" as it's also known, are sets of constantly developing theories that threaten many of the more accepted beliefs and dogmas about the process of human thinking. Books such as Carl Sagan's and Ann Druyan's *Shadows of Our Forgotten Ancestors*, Robert Wright's *The Moral Animal*, Jared Diamond's *The Third Chimpanzee*, and Desmond Morris's *Manwatching*, have convinced me that mankind is on the brink of major applications for this evolutionary approach to rationales for the human character.

DANIEL WATERS

SCREENPLAYS

Heathers (1989)

The Adventures of Ford Fairlane (1990), w/David Arnott and James Cappe

Hudson Hawk (1991), w/Steven De Souza

Batman Returns (1992)

Demolition Man (1993), w/Peter Lenkov and Rob Reneau

I get up at 7:33 A.M. every morning and have a slice of grapefruit along with three pieces of lightly browned toast. On Thursday, I allow myself bacon. I turn on my computer at 8:14 and complete two to two and half pages by lunch. During lunch, I take a red pencil and—I'm kidding, I mean, I am really, really kidding.

Regimentation personally scares the hell out of me. Having creatively contoured working hours is one of the pure pleasures of writing. I guess I can understand how it works for some people, but for me, regimented writing is like sitting on a toilet when you don't have to go to the bathroom, which is an apt metaphor considering some of my work.

For me, creative inspiration needs to be seductively snuck up on, not shoved against the wall and mugged. Viewing film is an act of the unconscious; writing them should be as well. Uh, okay, not exactly, but I just want to make it clear from the start that I'm one of the flakes. One of those scary people who think writing is cosmically more than plot points, act breaks, and emotional beats.

Everyone grows up with a biggest dream and a biggest fear. For as long as I could remember, I wanted to write the Great American Novel. That is to say, until I turned twelve. The summer before my thirteenth birthday, I saw *Jaws* (not the most esoteric epiphany, I know, but hey). I stood shivering in the lobby of the Scottsdale Theater of the Scottsdale Mall of South Bend, Indiana, knowing that I will still be a writer, but a writer in a medium that has an immediate, visceral effect upon a large community of people paying attention in a dark room. My biggest dream became becoming a screenwriter.

Oh, and as for the whole biggest-fear thing: I had a constant daymare about being wrongfully committed to a terrifying mental asylum. The natural response to being unfairly caged in such an institution would be to claw and screech in anger. But of course such action would make you seem more insane. The only possible way to get out of the snake pit would be to gulp down all your thoughts and emotions and pretend you really don't mind being abused because it's for your own good.

Twenty years later, I can reflect that I have realized my biggest dream . . . and my biggest fear. Alas, they are the same thing. Don't worry, I'm not going to go into some grandly masochistic rant—Oh hell, of course I am. . . .

The screenplay is the most fragile art form there is, the one with the most perilous journey from cocoon to butterfly. A novelist, a singer, a sculptor—they can just do it and it's done. I know that's a mighty simplification, but when a screenwriter "does it," it's not done—it's just begun. No one has to go through an uglier, middleman-packed, Chinese telephone torture than a screenwriter does—producers, directors, investors, studio executives, opinionated craft-services people. . . . I have never written a bad ending, yet every one of my films has one.

In order to protect your vision, you have to suppress your anger, your emotions, and your intelligence. Just like the sane guy trying to tiptoe out of the insane asylum, you have to strategically pick your battles.

The final irony is that, now more than ever, when a critic (professional and amateur) does not like a finished film, the first thing that gets blamed is the screenplay. Every writer has a tidy little Tale from the Crypt to underline their innocence loss. Here's mine:

Coming out of an opening-night screening of *Batman*, I remember huffing and puffing, "What amazing visuals—if only they had a decent script to work with." Imagine my smug glee when I was called upon to craft the sequel. I immediately locked myself away to incubate and hatch a nobly perverse little opus.

Like a pretty Midwestern freshman coed skipping upstairs into a fraternity gang-rape, my screenplay (to say nothing of me) casually/ quickly had its soul torn out by a variety of grinning demons, including

"Batman would never say that" studio heads, a visually oriented director deaf to my script's pleas for protection, and, finally, an "uncredited" writer brought in at the last minute to, in an executive's words, "make everything a little more normal"—a mission that involved the mind-numbing addition of kidnapped children and meaningless power plants.

Three years after seeing the first *Batman*, I emerge from an opening-night screening of "my" *Batman* (given the catchy title of *Batman Returns*). I hear a passing stranger sigh aloud, ". . . if only they had a decent script to work with . . ." Freeze frame on my howling face. Up with the Bernard Herrmann music. Cut back to Count Floyd.

From that moment on, I've tried to create the countermyth that the screenwriter should never be blamed. (I definitely owe the writer of the original *Batman* a hug.) You'll dutifully find me spouting such pearls as "I'll bet that zombie stripper movie had an amazing first draft. . . . the producer *made* the poor writer add that poisonously lame moment where the characters convulse into a sing-a-long of a Motown classic. . . . Surely the actor *ad-libbed*, 'I'm too old for this shit,' 'I got a ba-ad feeling,' and 'You can't fire me, I quit.' I mean, one of my brethren could not possibly write something that has been in forty-eight other movies."

Okay, okay, it's time to shut down the exploited screenwriter pity party. If only it were that simple. Desiring genocide is never a healthy thing, but there are way too many people that God intended to be math teachers, engineers, pediatricians, and telemarketers that have somehow weaseled their way into the film business because they think it's awesome.

This new breed loves the trappings of making movies with no real respect or affection for cinema itself. The Movies! The Industry! The Business! The Film Industry is like an amazing party that they just have to be a part of, so once they get into it, they can act bored and above it all.

An influx of deeply unimaginative people into the most imaginative medium there is. People determined to reduce the magic of celluloid into mundane terms their small minds can understand. I call these people Helluloids. They must die. Soon. In agony.

A Helluloid fast-forwards through a tape of *Casablanca* to find out what was being talked about at yesterday's meeting. Upon completion, the Helluloid huffs, "Well, it's no *Sleepless in Seattle*."

The first thing a Helluloid does when it gets a script is look at the last page so it can pout and whimper at the page number—"122 pages! No way! This is a joke, right?"

Helluloids love obsessing about page numbers and inflicting their own special brand of logical lifelessness: "We need conflict by page eight, some vulnerability around page fourteen, an unexpected revelation on page thirty-four, a moment of PG-13 sexuality around page fifty-nine, and a discrete fart joke by page eighty-eight . . ."

I wish I could report that the Helluloids are only readers and studio execs, but unfortunately, they have infested every position in Hollywood. Including Screenwriting. Especially screenwriting.

The position of director is still protected from the general public by certain mysteries like how to get DiCaprio to come out of his trailer and what's a filter? But the position of screenwriter—"It's just words and, man, I got a PowerBook! I have that new book *How to Write and Sell a Screenplay in Twelve Days* by that author who has never written or sold a screenplay in his life! Rock and Roll!"

The Helluloid has never stood shivering in the lobby of a theater deciding it wants to dedicate its life to writing movies. The Helluloid takes no joy in the process of writing. Writing to a Helluloid is a math problem that needs to be solved. A big video game involving the speedy juxtaposition of beloved clichés. The Remake is the Helluloid's ideal type of project.

The Helluloid screenwriter has been taught and trained to induce the birth of the baby as quickly as possible. Today's screenwriter wants to have the baby without falling in love and having sex, forgetting that love and sex are the best parts of the entire process.

The Helluloid never daydreams about the content of his work, about having an actual effect on an audience. It daydreams about opening weekend per-screen averages and hanging with Julia and Brad at the premiere.

Helluloid screenwriters chew more than they bite off. "Keep it simple" is their suffocating battle cry. Structure is not just everything, it is the only thing. Dialogue should never call attention to itself. Words are mere cogs in the almighty effort to keep the story moving forward. The perfect Helluloid script resembles three dominos stiffly set up behind each other then drably flicked over with a pinkie.

Oh, and God forbid there is an underlying ambition to "say something" in your work. That would be, dear me, "pretentious" (a word that had meaning pre-1980, but which has now become a verbal crutch for idiots—a trendy way of saying "I didn't get it," as if it was the art's fault, not the idiot's).

If the Helluloid screenwriter accidentally comes up with an element that has never been used in another movie, it does not rejoice, it becomes terrified, quickly burying this nugget of originality in the backyard with a shudder.

My mantra is write the greatest movie *never* made. Look to the films of the past as an enthralling place to evolve from, rather than a realm to repeat and repeat in endlessly lame necrophilia.

Come on, think! You must have a vision of a story or part of a story that excites you and that you have never quite seen before. For God's sake, write it. Do not worry about whether anyone else on the planet will like it.

Heathers was born from my desire to see a wiser and more subversive depiction of teenagers. I wrote entirely for myself; that others also had the need for a malevolently surreal vision of high school was a wonderful accident.

Don't obsess about coming up with an idea that "will sell"! Just as the light of a star you are beholding is probably from a planet that blew up a couple thousand years ago, when you think you've detected a trend, it's probably already over.

So go ahead, create a male lead who is a chain-smoking gay who hates to practice safe sex when making love to the President. Create a female character who is not of the deadly dull, sanctimonious, "I-*am*-Doctor-Johnson!"—"But-you're-a-*woman!*" variety, but rather one who is strange, fucked-up, and actually allowed to deliver a funny line of dialogue or two. A "tough" female is easy to write; to write one that is witty is revolutionary. Oh, while you're at it, how about an unhappy ending!

The first draft is the one thing they can't take away from you, so revel in it. Don't let anyone tell you that the most important part is the mechanics of it all. The most important part is the initial daydream. If you write a stunningly unique personal mind-blower, you may not sell it right away, but you will get attention. Your name will go on that sanctified list of Talented People To Be Exploited.

The delightful irony is that most studios are sickened by writers who openly pander to perceived mainstream tastes. Helluloids despise other Helluloids; they love people with original visions (not to mention the tingling challenge of turning these people into Helluloids like themselves).

Whew, after all this bitterness, I owe everyone a joke: How many screenwriters does it take to change a light bulb?

"'Change the light bulb?'—That's the best part!"

TREY ELLIS

SCREENPLAYS

The Inkwell (1994) as "Tom Ricostranza," w/Paris Qualles

The Tuskegee Airmen, cable telefeature (1995), w/Ron Hutchinson
and Paris Qualles

NOVELS

Platitude (1988)

Home Repairs (1992)

Right Here Right Now (1999)

At thirty-five, I've been a professional screenwriter and novelist for more than a decade. I've already experienced some breathtaking ups and downs, tastes and nibbles of fame and folly, and I'm only at the close of my career's first act! I guess that, more than anything, is what my decade in Hollywood has taught me—that the ground is never solid between Santa Monica and the Valley. That here, the corporate ladder is a roller coaster. Added all up it makes for an eventful, unforgettable life.

I wrote my first movie in the sixth grade. Mike Zegans and I wrote a twenty-page comedy about some rich kids in a summer camp. I think I still have a few pages of it, somewhere. I took my first creative-writing course in the eleventh grade at Phillips Academy, Andover, and a month later submitted a short story to *The New Yorker*. A week later they sent back a pre-printed rejection slip.

At Stanford I majored in creative writing and edited the campus humor magazine, *The Stanford Chaparrel*. All of us at the magazine dreamed of nothing but one day writing for *Saturday Night Live*, and I personally must have written hours of sample comedy sketches. I assumed I'd graduate, make a few phone calls, and presto! I'd be pulling down thousands a week for staying up late and writing gags with my friends.

My dad, on the other hand, was convinced I'd graduate college with no marketable skills and end up jobless and back at home for the better half of the Eighties. To please him, I applied for a summer internship at *Newsweek*. I quickly discovered that I liked journalism and figured I could make an honorable living—still with a pen—even if I were not completely true to following my bliss.

However, before completely shelving my dream, I decided to give myself one last year of freedom. After graduating I spent a few months trying to land any sort of TV writing job whatsoever. Then, licking my wounds, I returned to Florence, Italy, where I'd done a school year abroad. There, for another year, I extended a short story I began in college into *Platitudes*, my first novel.

I returned to New York and worked as a proofreader for *Rolling Stone* and *Interview* while trying to sell my novel and write a spec script. The novel eventually sold to Random House, and a small production company paid me five thousand dollars to adapt an off-Broadway musical to the screen. That money doubled my annual salary that year, and the producer submitted the script to The Sundance Film Institute. It turned out to be one of the best experiences of my life.

The institute's mentors such as Tom Rickman, Frank Pierson, Richard Price, Ring Lardner, Jr., and Terry Southern created the single-most inspiring creative working atmosphere I'd ever known. They really showed me that just as much care and craft can go into writing films as into fiction. I left the Screenwriter's Lab on a cloud, convinced that all my days and nights in and around Hollywood would be as rosy.

The Inkwell, a coming-of-age comedy, was the story of my adolescence. *The Summer of '42* has always been one of my favorite films, and somehow I got the idea of writing a comedy about a black teen spending the summer on Martha's Vineyard who falls in love with an older woman. He knows there's no way on Earth she will ever sleep with him until the day he sees *The Summer of '42*. Suddenly, he's inspired! If only the woman's husband would die, and if the boy could time it so he'd be there to comfort her, then *presto*!, just like in the movie, she'd throw him on the bed and end the misery of his virginity.

I'd spent most of my own young summers in Oak Bluffs, a black, middle-class enclave on Martha's Vineyard, and decided to set the film in 1976 to play off the Bicentennial and '70's-styled fashions. It took me three months to write the kooky, black comedy, and I really didn't expect it to sell. But Touchstone bought the film for me to direct, and suddenly my phone was ringing off the hook as if they were confusing me for Spike Lee. All the studio asked for was a quick little director's test, one day of shooting, just to make sure I wasn't some sort of lunatic. I guess I was some sort of lunatic because they took my wistful, bourgeois black comedy away from me and gave it to Matty Rich, then the twenty-something self-educated director of a film called *Straight Outta Brooklyn*. Touchstone said they wanted to give it a gritty, urban edge. I took my name off my film.

The Inkwell disaster was a hard and public lesson to learn. It was also the first time I can ever remember seriously failing. When *Platitudes* came out I was 26, then the youngest published novelist in the country. (I know 'cause I compulsively checked the back flap of every new book.) With *The Inkwell* I was twenty-nine and ready to add "director" to my wunderkind crown. I hadn't worked up my roller coaster metaphor yet since my career thus far had been one sure and steady ascent, so the no-handed screaming ride to the bottom of that first big hill was quite a shock.

I rose again when one of the very first scripts I ever wrote, *The Tuskegee Airmen*, was brought out of turnaround from Columbia Pictures to HBO. HBO made it a year later starring Lawrence Fishburne, John Lithgow, and Cuba Gooding, Jr. It was then nominated for an Emmy for Outstanding Writing in a Miniseries or Special.

I finished another novel, *Home Repairs*, and I settled into a writerly routine that I can only describe as Edenic. I write from ten till two, then surf or take a yoga class, have coffee with one of my fellow goldbricking writer friends. My wife and I spend the month of August in the south of France. It's a balancing act, living like the upper class on an upper-middle-class salary, but screenwriting is one of the only jobs in the world that can open that door.

Things got a little less Edenic, the balancing act tipped a little more than I would have liked, a few years ago. My *modus operandi* had been to write a few screenplays, save up my money, then take several months off to write fiction. I guess I hadn't saved as much as I thought because just as I was finishing a draft of my newest novel, *Right Here, Right Now,* I realized I was fast approaching financial ruin. My wife and I looked around our lovely Santa Monica Canyon home, and The Doors' song "This Is the End" kept echoing in my brain. Then I was inspired! I wrote a spec comedy about an upper-middle-class couple's plummet to the working class. Suddenly, Goldie Hawn, fresh off of *The First Wives' Club,* was begging to attach herself. Suddenly, agents I'd never even heard of at my agency were calling me up just to chitchat. I kept promising myself that I wouldn't change after the 1.5 million-dollar check was messengered over.

"Goldie's out," my agent told me a day later on the phone. "She won't say why."

C'est la vie.

Fortunately, soon thereafter my wife sold her first novel, *Good Fences*, to Random House. I sold *Right Here, Right Now* to Simon & Schuster.

Finally, I noticed that race colors the perception of me in the film community today much more than I would have thought a decade ago. I call it my "Lion Theory." Being black in Hollywood sometimes feels like being a lion. You might think of yourself as a happy lion, an over-educated lion, a fat lion, a lion in a Donna Karan suit, but as soon as you enter a room, all the creative exec seems to see are teeth and mane. That is not to say that I feel they are afraid of being eaten or menaced in any way, just that that one fact about me often seems to totally eclipse all others.

Where I see this played out most baldly is in the scripts I am most often offered. The studio will say they just read my supposedly arty, nuanced spec script about an interracial love affair set in the '50s, say they are aware I am also a novelist and journalist, then ask me if I'd like to do a quick polish of *Booty Call: The Revenge*. At times like that, if I were really a beast prowling the Serengetti, I'd be tempted to bite a quick chunk out of somebody's leg.

I haven't always loved Hollywood, but I've always loved roller coasters. It wasn't till I realized they were one and the same that I found peace here. And peace in Hollywood is something that is often very well hidden. Now, I don't know what I'd do with a regular job and a steady paycheck. These ups and downs and middles make every day an adventure. And an adventure a day is a wonderful way to find inspiration for that next story to tell.

MICHAEL GRAIS

SCREENPLAYS

Death Hunt (1981), w/Mark Victor

Poltergeist (1982), w/Steven Spielberg and Mark Victor

Poltergeist II: The Other Side (1986), w/Mark Victor

Marked for Death (1990), w/Mark Victor

Cool World (1992), w/Mark Victor

I was born on Easter Sunday in Illinois. My first memories are of being alone and in danger. I had a drug and alcohol problem that started when I was nine years old. I'd steal my mother's yellow sleeping pills from the medicine cabinet we shared. I'd sleep for twenty-four hours. Relief from a life I found both boring and terrifying. I was raised Jewish. I loved Jesus. I believed he was the son of God.

The nightmares had already begun to disturb my sleep. They had gotten so bad and predictable that going to bed at night was something I'd dread. Most nights I'd end up in my sister's bed sobbing and shaking. She'd hold me and I'd go to sleep. My parents had long ago started to lock their bedroom door at night so that I couldn't seek comfort from them.

Myrtle Simms, a 200-pound black woman from the South, was my surrogate mother. They called her a maid. My real mother was bedridden with manic depression. Between spells of abuse and chaos or charm and sociability, I knew where to find her.

Myrtle taught me about cooking, sex, crazy white people, and drinking. She'd let me drive Mom's '59 Plymouth Fury convertible to Pat

Patterson's liquor store, where she'd disappear for an hour or so, doing what I could only imagine inside the dark one-story ramshackle building. But when she'd return to the car looking flushed, she'd have my reward. A half pint of Seagram's 7. I liked the feel of the bottle. The color of the liquor. The hot taste. But most of all . . . the relief. I belonged to the group who longed for that relief. I belonged somewhere. I was eleven years old.

"Boy, you're so bad, someday they're gonna put your ass *under* the jail," Myrtle would laugh. I was one mad pre-teenage alcoholic driving a big, fast convertible, smoking a cigarette with my pal, whom I loved, a black woman from someplace called "The South." Life seemed as slow as tar.

I escaped not only through alcohol and drugs, but in drawing, painting, toy soldiers, and movies. *The Wild One*, starring a leather-clad Marlon Brando, gave me an identity. I began wearing a motorcycle jacket, blue jeans, combat boots, and putting Vaseline in my hair. My bicycle became my Harley. My friends became my gang. I was always in trouble. Teachers suspected I was "slow."

One day, I wrote a short story for English class. I was in sixth grade. As I wrote it, I felt the sentences pouring out of me with unsuspected power. The story was about the last thoughts of a German soldier in World War I before his unit stormed a farmhouse full of enemy soldiers and he was killed. The story contained a "ticking clock" as his sergeant counted down the seconds to the assault.

The story stunned the teacher, my parents, and myself. They quickly reevaluated my condition from "slow" to underachiever. They gave me books I liked to read. My interest in writing was born.

I started dating Leslie when she was fourteen and I was a year older. She was skinny and sexy and pretty. She liked sex, she liked teasing and flirting, and she liked me enough to be my girlfriend. I liked her more than alcohol. She became my drug. She blossomed into something resembling a Playboy Bunny, and every young stud around wanted a piece of her action. She tortured me with her flirtations. I was consumed with lust, rage, and jealousy. We stayed together until I left for college on the east coast, and even in my freshman year, we still saw each other once in a while.

With her gone, I returned to my first love, drugs. I discovered methamphetamine and pot. I started writing with a passion. I conversed with God. I was invincible. Insane. Enlightened. Half the school was stoned on something. It was the '60s. All that great music, free pussy, cheap dope, and war.

But what was I going to do with my life? How could I survive? The Army wanted me in Vietnam. The answer came while I was watching Antonioni's *Blow Up*. It was obvious! I'd become a photographer and meet pretty models. I'd go to film school. Keep my deferment. Stay alive. But first, I went to Peru for six months and took photographs, fell in love twice, chewed coca leaves, and played the drums.

I'd been at NYU Film School for three years when I was requested to join the armed forces of the United States in its holy war against the yellow people. I was told by an anti-war lawyer that if I caused enough trouble at the induction center, there was a good chance they'd let me go. But I had to prove I'd be more trouble than I was worth. Which meant that I'd be dead before I could be of any use whatsoever and the U.S. Government would have wasted their investment in training and clothes and food and housing.

I flunked the IQ test with flying colors. My drawings of demons and genitalia on the test sheet assured me a visit with the shrink. I weighed 129 pounds and had hair to my shoulders à la Jim Morrison. I wore black suede pants, a black T-shirt, and a leather jacket all the time. I was an alcoholic, a drug addict, a manic-depressive, and I believed I fooled the shrink into letting me go. He told me, "Don't worry, son, we're not going to take you. You can go home."

The only problem was I couldn't find the door to get out. A friendly sergeant escorted me to the street. I knew something was wrong inside my brain, but I also knew I wasn't going to have that brain blown out in Vietnam. I took the Staten Island ferry round-trip and lay on the deck thanking God I was alive.

It was 1971. I decided to go to Nazareth in Israel to a Kibbutz. A war was going on there and they needed volunteers to pick fruit. I needed a place to recover. Some people go to Graceland. I go to Nazareth.

I picked fruit in 120-degree heat. I watched bombs drop in the distance. In the afternoons I swatted flies, smoked hash, slept in a pool of sweat. I had sex with a drunken German girl named Ula. I went to the old City of Jerusalem. I was banned from the Holy Sepulcher of Jesus Christ for having long hair and no shoes. I traveled on to Greece and lived in a hut on a nude beach but always wore my bathing suit. I took acid and went to the beach where everyone wore bathing suits and they watched me get naked and swim laughing. I took a Russian ship to Spain and met teenagers who were terrified of the State Police and hungry for Beatles music. In Spain, the cops clubbed hippies in the cafés, so I split for Ibiza and finally Formentera, where I wrote a 344-page screenplay with my boyhood pal, Mark. We drank absinthe like Rimbaud and bought drugs over the counter. I read Castaneda at night until paralyzed from the neck down by some wonder drug called "dormidinas." (No nightmares while on those babies.) Friends started dying from the effects of drugs back home. My pals didn't die in rice paddies but in crash pads. One died of a heroin overdose, one from the effects of LSD, one from a suicidal bullet. I had an affair with an actress from the Canadian cast of *Hair*. She was beautiful, bisexual, and had cancer. I don't know if she survived it.

I moved to Boston. Wrote poetry. Listened to Bessie Smith and Rod Stewart's Gasoline Alley while snorting cocaine, drinking bourbon, and dating coeds. I met my future ex-wife, Michele. I saw my first ghost in a haunted house on Beacon Hill. I embezzled money, drove a purple Firebird, fell in love with Michele, graduated from college. I left Michele and went back to Greece. Left Greece and went overland to India. Left India for Nepal. I trekked the footpath to China. I meditated in the Himalayas and looked for God in those majestic peaks. I ran with Sherpas at night who carried torches to light our way.

I walked alone for days, weeks, months, a year. I went from Ashram to Ashram and temple to temple. I went back to India. I met my Doppelganger in the marketplace in Benares, a Sadu wearing an orange lungi and carrying a cane. We sat together and watched people being cremated on the banks of the river Ganges for days and nights. I saw spirits in the sky. I came to believe in life after death. I understood Maya.

I returned to the United States after a vision told me it was time to return and discovered Michele had gone nuts while she was in Afghanistan on a drug run and I was in India searching for God or Buddha or myself. She had transformed herself into a gypsy. She inhabited a dark, sensual, angry place that attracted stray lunatics of all varieties to our door. She kicked me out and I went to Chicago and worked for my father, who'd had a severe heart attack while I was gone. He put me to work in his factory, in the back, where I wouldn't offend anyone with my long hair, beard, and earring. We began to drink together and became friends.

I cut off my beard, threw away the earring, bought some platform shoes, designer jeans, a white Camaro, and tried to fit in. I remember the day my Dad and I were drinking shots of bourbon at Gene & Georgetti's steak house and I was hyped and rapping a mile a minute. He looked at me with sudden understanding. "Oh, I get it," he said. "You're nuts." I had to agree. I quit the job, went to graduate school, sold the Camaro, bought a pickup truck, talked Michele into living with me on a country road in Eugene, Oregon. We got a cat named Fred; I wore a cowboy hat and drank a lot. The nightmares got worse. Poetry almost killed me. It was so damp my guns rusted under the bed.

I graduated with an MFA, sold the truck, and we drove to L.A. in Michele's Volvo. I'd decided I'd try to make a living as a writer. Michele had an uncle who owned a store in Beverly Hills. He was our only contact. We parked our car on Rodeo Drive with all our possessions inside and stepped out into the bright California sunshine. We wore jeans, work boots, plaid shirts. Everyone around us wore Spandex and gold chains. Men carried purses.

"Michael, is that you?"

I looked up and saw Leslie, my high-school sweetheart, swaying out of Theodore's, where she worked as a salesgirl. Disco music seemed to follow her like a soundtrack. It was 1974.

Michele looked at me, and I should've known right then the trouble was only starting. Hollywood, man, *nothing* prepares you for this ride.

Mr. Grais has been clean and sober for fifteen years. Sleep is still elusive.

JEFF
ARCH

SCREENPLAYS

Sleepless in Seattle (1993), w/Nora Ephron and David S. Ward

Iron Will (1984), w/John Michael Hayes and Djordje Milicevic

Santa Monica. 1978. I'm twenty-three years old, at a friend's apartment while I look for my own place. The phone rings. It's my uncle, my father's brother, who tracked me down because he thought it was time to tell me something my father never told me while he was alive: how their father, my grandfather, left Russia. "Everyone was going west, through Europe," my uncle said. "But Pop went east."

Now, east meant all the way across Russia. And then somehow across the water that divides their continent from ours, and into America. Then, somehow again, all the way across America to Pennsylvania, where he stopped and settled into a community with other refugees who came the "normal" way and who must have really wondered about him.

I think my uncle told me this, and chose the time, because he heard that I had decided to move to California and write movies. Maybe my mom called him, all freaked out about my chances. I know she thought it was crazy, if inevitable, that I was even going to try. So it wouldn't be out of line for her to get my uncle to stand in for my father and say something manly to me. But however it came about, I know that when he told me this story, I suddenly felt like I had a secret weapon. The whole enterprise was just as impossible, and there were too many times when that story was all I had—but at least I had it.

Because the lesson I took was this: not that craziness runs in the family, but that *the man didn't care how much harder it was—he just didn't want to do what everybody else was doing.* He was willing to go that far out to have things fit the way he saw them, and he had what it took to make it.

And that's what was in my blood.

Virginia. 1990. I'm thirty-five years old, married with two very young kids. No one's asking, but I get an idea for a love story where the two main characters don't even meet until the very last scene—but that when they do, it's on top of the Empire State Building, on Valentine's Day. I call it *Sleepless in Seattle*, and I know it's going to be a monster. I can feel it.

Every single person I tell this to says that I'm out of my mind. "That's not how you do love stories," they say. "You do them *this* way." And, "What kind of *title* is that?"

My grandfather's wilderness was physical. Mine was emotional. But we both had the same secret weapon.

DANA STEVENS

SCREENPLAYS

Blink (1994)

City of Angels (1998)

I have an office in Santa Monica. A little room above some shops; four walls and green carpeting and two windows overlooking the parking lot. I rented it late last year in a fiat, wading through the middle of the worst writer's block I've ever had. There are only a few things in here. A desk, a twenty-dollar lamp with anthuriums painted on it from the Rose Bowl Swap Meet, a boom box, and a ridiculously expensive ergonomic chair. I got a bulletin board and pinned things on it; pictures of the places I was writing about, a photo of a fashionably strung-out Kate Moss that inspired me with her haunted look. But the first month in the office didn't solve my writer's block at all. In fact, it made it worse. I felt that this little room was a prison—no kitchen, no garden, no telephone. People talking in the hallways. I grew to hate it with almost paranoiac fear. So I went back to my home office, now a mess, and minus my special chair. I floated from room to room in my house, trying to get comfortable, trying to write. Finally, I went to the San Ysidro Ranch, a very posh hotel in Santa Barbara. I worked outside on the front porch of my little cottage. I got a massage. I swam in the pool and walked on the beach and visited a Buddhist temple. And still I cried and cursed and struggled through the script.

The truth of the matter is, I couldn't solve my block with location. Or silence or self-flagellation. I could only let myself off the hook. My block was about my own ego as much as anything. I had become my worst critic: a one-woman, pissed-off audience. I was writing for myself alone, trying to please this harsh task-master, and I had forgotten the primary reason we write or make movies or do any of this. COMMU-NICATION. We are trying to communicate—to other people. So I came back to my little office, which, after all, I had leased for a year. Someone had broken in and stolen my boom box. No matter; Radio Shack is right down the street. So I got a new deadbolt and a new boom box, and I turned my chair away from the windows. And I pinned something on the bulletin board, a message, over the maps of Grenada and haunted Kate Moss, and it was this:

Tell Us A Story

Tell us a story. That's all. Who's us? I don't know. But someone other than the aforementioned me. Writing is like dreaming. Like a kid who has to go to bed when he doesn't want to, the writer has to go write. So he (or she) bitches and whines and wanders around and "circles" the task at hand. He sits in the chair and can't think of anything, like the kid who lays in bed trying to make himself sleep and gets all panicky and annoyed. And then suddenly, without even knowing when or how, the writer is asleep . . . he has drifted into R.E.M. He is actually *writing* and not trying to write anymore, and he looks up at his watch and hours have passed. Like the kid who wakes up and realizes he did in fact sleep. That ergonomic chair has become like a cradle to me. I sit in it and it suspends me like an astronaut. The little office is almost like a deprivation chamber. I put my earphones on and listen to music. Before I start any project, I make a tape, or maybe two, of music that inspires me, that approximates the tone of the movie I'm trying to write. So I have the music and the chair and the sun on my back, and I essentially fall asleep.

When I first started writing, I was a struggling actress, living on Hayworth Avenue, in a grungy little apartment behind Peanuts, the lesbian discotheque. My former boyfriend, now a successful writer, had helped me acquire gainful employment as a script reader at fifty bucks a pop. Several mornings, maybe one or two a month, I would awaken to the sound of someone playing a tenor sax. Once again, my view was of other people's parking lots, but I also had a tree. And the sunlight would dapple in through the leaves and I would hear that mournful, beautiful sax . . . I built quite a fantasy life around the man playing that sax, but then it occurred to me, as I eyeballed everyone on the street, that the sax player might in fact be an old guy, or a woman, or a jerk. And that is how my first screenplay was born. What if . . .

I wrote it blithely, with youthful enthusiasm, sometimes pounding out fifteen or twenty pages in an evening. It never got produced. But I long for that freedom now, that belief in myself. How did I get so botched up? Thinking about what the actors will and won't say, thinking about what is cool and what is stupid, thinking about what is cliché. The truth is, I am a much better writer now than I was then because I do question myself, relentlessly. The writer does have to have a third eye, an instinctual sense of what people will respond to and when the scene should end and when you've said too much. But to create, one has to tell the third eye to shut up, at least in the beginning, or it will destroy you.

When I was a kid I had these fantastic old volumes of *Grimm's Fairy Tales*. One of the stories is called "One Eye, Two Eyes, Three Eyes," about two ugly sisters who tortured the pretty one (Two Eyes). The illustration of these three is really the stuff of nightmares. Whenever I think of the third eye that has plagued me as an actress and a writer, I think of that chick in her medieval, pointy hat. The three sisters planted a tree that yielded golden apples. But One Eye couldn't pick the apples, because she couldn't see well enough, and Three Eyes couldn't either, because her three eyes gave her swimming, double vision. Only Two Eyes could get the golden apple, and—by the way—the Prince, too. But that's another story.

As I become what is termed a successful writer, I find myself distracted from the pure joy of examination and imagination. I write for the details, the little moments in life that make me wonder about others and their stories. And I write to live in another world, the world where I get the guy, and he always says the most amazing, perfect thing and, lo and behold, so do I. That's, I suppose, why we go to the movies as well. To escape. To become something else. In my younger days, after certain intense movies, I would get outside, into the real world, still so involved in the story I had just seen that I would be surprised to see my own reflection in a passing window. I thought I might see Tim Hutton or Meryl Streep staring back at me. After *Goodfellas*, I thought everyone walking toward me was going to shoot me. After *The Player*, everyone outside the theater seemed like stereotype Hollywood hipsters—well, actually, they were, but you get the gist. Movies take us away. They make us laugh and weep and want so badly to really *live*. Like novels do, or plays, or great music—it's all one. That's why the arts are important. Why, after observing an open-heart surgery as research for *City of Angels*, I didn't kill myself for doing the worthless job I do. Because the surgeon, and the guy on the table whose heart I saw beating in his chest, and the nurses and technicians, they love the movies. They want and need to be transported. Life would be so dull without stories. It's such a human thing, telling a good story. And every now and then I get a glimpse—that I might in my minuscule way be a part of that great tradition. And for that, I am grateful, and honored, to sit in my space-man chair and dream.

JOHN
BRANCATO

SCREENPLAYS

Femme Fatale (1991) w/Michael Ferris
Into the Sun (1992) w/Michael Ferris
Interceptor (1993) w/Michael Ferris
The Net (1995) w/Michael Ferris
The Game (1997) w/Michael Ferris

"**H**ow do you get your ideas?" This has to be the question writers get asked most often (other than, "Are you ready to order?"). I usually answer with something flippant like, "Steal them from *you*." But for once I'll attempt to recall honestly how I got me one.

"*The Player* movie idea" appears for the date August 18, 1991, in my "This Day in History" calendar. The entry is circled in the same color ink (black), but I added the circle a month or more later. Also on 8/18/91: "Wash cat. Clean outdoors. Pay bills. Take-out Chinese. *I, Claudius.*" On that date in 1587, says the calendar, "Virginia Dare is the first person of English parentage born in America."

It was a lifeless, hot Sunday morning. I was sitting in a stained white Ikea chair in front of the living-room picture window, ignoring the gray-beige panorama of Hollywood. My wife was in the breakfast room, reading the Sunday L.A. *Times*, which usually occupied her until late afternoon. I'd spent most of the day chasing a new puppy around our ugly little rented house, snatching him up before he could piss on the brown shag carpeting. I was sticky with sweat, my breathing was cramped, and my mouth tasted bad. I'd smoked too many cigarettes and drunk too much wine the night before, staying up late playing bridge. My coffee was lukewarm, oily droplets of fat left by the turning half-and-half glistened on its surface.

I was dreading yet another enervating and hopeless studio meeting, this one at Fox about developing a vehicle for a Brat Pack actor (one not that hot at the time, and since ever colder). My writing partner, Mike Ferris, and a college friend of his turned director were also involved. Two weeks before, a Fox D-girl had pitched the three of us a tale of an ennui-drenched, born-rich playboy drawn into a web of nuclear blackmail and espionage . . . a sort of *Notorious*, with the Brat Packer as Ingrid Bergman. Complete shit, but we were all hungry enough to eat it and say it tasted good. An audience with the boy king actor himself was now scheduled for the coming week. So, I asked myself, what might transform a dissolute Monte Carlo jet-setter into a conscientious Uzi-toting defender of democracy? I know! I'll tell them I have pneumonia and blow if off.

I'd started writing for film in 1985; a half-dozen B features and a handful of TV episodes had been produced. That summer I'd begun fantasizing about moving to Maine and becoming a teacher. Of course I hated movies and show business, but what I hated most was my collaboration with the enemy. Other than inertia, what kept me from a virtuous life in the north woods was the feeling that I'd never really given it my best shot. All I'd written were cynical attempts to give the world what it wanted . . . I'd never written what *I* wanted.

Like the imaginary Brat Pack hero, I was bored. Since I was nearly broke, I had the luxury of pretending that money would solve everything. I also knew this was bullshit, that my boredom was a mask for frustration and self-loathing . . . but that little insight didn't help much when I was ready to pluck every hair from my body just for the change it might produce.

I forced my thoughts to drift, anything is better than trying to come up with movie ideas. I thought about a cure for boredom. So-called entertainment was a symptom, not a solution. Suicide had always struck me as a potent remedy, but I'd already spent thirty years postponing it, figuring I could always die tomorrow, and by then it might happen by itself and I wouldn't have to go to all the trouble. No, getting what you thought you wanted wasn't a cure, it would only make it worse. Besides, boredom is made out of not-wanting, of not recognizing what's lacking . . . or that anything is lacking. One thing was certain: If a cure existed, a truly bored man might pay any price.

Eureka! (I don't only apply the word after the fact, the idea exploded in my head with the force of revelation.) A service exists that promises only one thing: you won't be bored. A client approaches them—no, they approach a client—then they study the subject for a while in order to figure out just how to keep him or her from being bored. How? Well . . . that would vary, depending on the individual's needs. Experience design, yeah . . . but more than that, you'd have to change the subject himself, change him all the way to his core. Shatter him, fuck his mind, drive him insane. I'd been insane, and while it wasn't exactly fun, at least it wasn't boring.

This imaginary company couldn't let on how it works, just that it works. The mystery is part of the sales pitch. They take the rich guy, surprise him, amuse him for a while—they play God. It could take the form of a game. He keeps trying to figure it out, while the game keeps getting weirder and more dangerous. He can't tell what's real anymore, his whole world is turned upside down and inside out (which is exactly what he wanted, although he didn't know it). And just when things look worst, they pull back the curtain and reveal it all to be what it was at the beginning: a joke. The cure is that there is no cure, heaven and hell are right next door to each other, they're the same place. Wow, an organic, existentially correct yet unexpected happy ending. And a strong, never-used title (I ran to check Leonard Maltin): *The Player*.

The more I thought about it, the more excited I became. This was more than a good idea, it was a great idea. It could actually make for a genuinely cool movie. Dumb and smart, the same but different, surprising yet obvious . . . eek, it felt too obvious, it had to exist out there already. I was pacing now as I scanned my cranial database. Movies: reminiscent of *The Sting* and '60's acid-tinged paranoia like *Seconds* or *The Tenth Victim*, but not exactly. Books: akin to Fowles' *The Magus* or Chesterton's *The Man Who Was Thursday*, but just a little. (Months later, a friend sent me a copy of a G.K. Chesterton short story I'd never read about a rich person's surprise club, which was indeed similar.) I tore my wife Jennifer away from the Calendar section. She liked the idea, happy to see my extreme passion for it, and she couldn't come up with a fatal precedent.

I called Mike Ferris that afternoon, the thing was already becoming an obsession. He got it instantly, and pointed out why I'd felt such strong déjà vu: "It's Phool's Week." The game was like a souped-up version of a collegiate initiation ritual we'd both undergone. For five sleep-deprived days, you're made to walk around on your knees, perform stupid pranks, memorize poetry and pornographic song lyrics, and dance in the streets in the hopes of being elected to membership. Goofiness alternates with serious psychological cruelty. Finally they shove you out the door and tell you you're rejected . . . only to pull you back inside to celebrate your election with a wild, drunken formal party. Later that night, you receive a bill for the initiation and first month's dues.

Mike and I immediately began to elaborate the game itself, conjuring plunging cars and leaps from great heights. The story felt cohesive and movielike; it even fit that soul-deadening three-act paradigm. We pitched it to the Brat Packer as scheduled (he was too hung over to say much but seemed to like it), and to a junior Fox exec soon after, on August 26. "That could be a *great* movie," the exec said the moment we'd finished. Uh-oh. "Interesting . . . very imaginative, very original." The use of any one of these three adjectives in a development meeting means, "I hate it." He passed on the spot, which almost never happens.

In the immortal words of Robert Evans, "Fuck 'em, fuck 'em all." We started writing the script the next morning. I hardly slept during the next ten days. When I did, I dreamt scenes from the script. I spent most every waking moment at the computer, unable to think or talk about anything else. We finished a rough draft on September 5. I liked it. If it didn't sell, well, that was okay—I'd know I was in the wrong business, and could leave Hollywood with no regrets.

No such luck. A spec sale and six years of heart-breaking, game-like reversals ensued, a bottomless pit of rejections, options, turnarounds, back-burners, green lights, red lights, compromises, tantrums, betrayals, firings, hirings, lawsuits . . . and no fewer than eleven rewrites, by the end of which the script was back pretty much where it started.

As I write this, the movie is a few weeks away from its premiere. I just saw the final cut. The most astonishing thing about *The Game* is that it's entirely true to the original idea. If anyone should happen to ask how I got that idea, I think I'd better just say it was a visitation from the Muse.

JOHN BRILEY

SCREENPLAYS

Invasion Quartet (1961), w/Jack Trevor Story

Postman's Knock (1961), w/Jack Trevor Story

Children of the Damned (1964)

Pope Joan (1972)

That Lucky Touch (1975)

The Medusa Touch (1978)

Eagle's Wing (1979)

Gandhi (1982)

Enigma (1983)

Marie (1985)

Tai-Pan (1986), w/Stanley Mann

Cry Freedom (1987)

Like most people who began writing for films when I did, I came to the profession by accident. (Film schools were for the next decade.) I had written and directed for the stage, again largely by accident, and was hired by the head of MGM (Britain), who had seen some of the shows I'd written.

I was in England to get a Ph.D. The idea was, I would get my doctorate, then be able to get a job at an American university. (I was born in Kalamazoo, Michigan, and dreamed I would spend most of my adult life outside the United States.) The university job would enable me to eat while I wrote "the great American novel"—or any novel . . . my secret ambition from the time I was about eleven.

I had received my doctorate in Elizabethan Drama. Mostly because I had a great professor from England (G.B. Harrison) who made me love Shakespeare and was my avenue to a British university, where another mentor (Allan Seager) told me any self-respecting writer in the English language had to spend at least a year.

I never dreamed of writing drama. Only Arthur Miller, Tennessee

Williams, and William Inge seemed to be able to make a living from it, and I knew there were thousands of would-be playwrights in universities all over America. I studied Shakespeare only as a means of getting the degree.

But after I finished my residence requirements in Stratford, I found I could do active duty for the U.S. Air Force in Europe, buying food, booze, and unbelievable goodies at the PXs at prices any poor student would die for.

They didn't really care what you did for this "reserve duty," and since I had been an emcee on an industrial show for General Motors while I was an undergraduate at the University of Michigan, they suggested I spend my two weeks writing a show for the military in England. The Armed Forces Network wasn't allowed to broadcast there because it was English language and the BBC didn't want the competition of American shows. Theoretically the troops were therefore starved for American entertainment.

So—spending much of my time in the PX—I wrote a comedy show about Americans (whom I knew) and the English (whom I'd come to know). By accident it was June, the end of the Air Force's fiscal year. A couple of people read my script, thought it half-way funny, and said, why not do another two weeks in the new financial year and direct it. It meant being paid again, and being able to use the PX again. So I did it.

By yet another accident, the ranking general happened to visit a remote base when the show was playing there. Outside was mud and rain, the morale was terrible. Inside the base theater a collection of the troops were pounding their feet, laughing and cheering this bunch of itinerants I had put together from GIs and unemployed English actors. (One GI was Larry Hagman, and several of the Englishmen went on to become very famous and rich in their own country.) The general thought the show was great for the rank and file and, through his minions, made me an offer far beyond my expectations as an academic to stay and write and direct more.

I did. And from that went on to write a comedy series for the BBC and one for ITV, wrote and directed two comedies on the stage in London, and got the offer to write for MGM. It made me believe all those years of studying Shakespeare had somehow taught me more about drama than I ever realized.

I remained in England for a couple of decades. During that time I worked with many famous actors and many famous directors. I won an Academy Award for *Gandhi*, a couple of Christopher Awards (*Cry Freedom, Marie*), and even managed to write a couple of novels (*The Traitors*, something the *Chicago Sun-Times* called "the best fiction to come out of Vietnam," and *The Last Dance*).

I had my down times, the times most writers have, wondering if you'll ever sell anything again, damning yourself for not being a lawyer or bus driver or something sensible, but by and large it was a fulfilling time that gave me the money to eat (and then some), often a great sense of pride, and a life of continual interest and learning.

I came to realize that what others had said about films being the medium of the twentieth century was true, and that it had been my good fortune to fall into a profession where my work would be seen and responded to by all—in the way Shakespeare's work had. You wrote for everyone, the groundlings and the gods. And if you wanted to make some impact, there was no better way for a writer to do so. And despite its egalitarian nature, I felt "the trade" gave me a certain sense of dignity, too.

Then, recently, I came back to America.

It started long ago in the Depression when writers in Hollywood, in order to guarantee they would be paid by some of the scoundrels running the business, elected to make themselves "employees"—thereby getting the protection of the law for their "wages," but at the same time giving up their copyrights to the producer or company who hired them.

In America a screenplay is not the writer's property. It belongs to whoever contracts to pay him—whether they pay him or not is irrelevant, he or she has still signed away the copyright. The writer's mental product has therefore come to be treated by the studios as raw material to be "improved" by a bureaucracy of wanna-bes who have never made anyone laugh or cry, whose knowledge of writing comes from script gurus who have never written either but who teach them the "rules" of drama. If you ever wonder how so many horrendous formula pictures come from overpaid Hollywood, look not to the writers, but to the system.

And since the copyright does not belong to the writer, a powerful producer, director, or actor can take the raw material already sausaged by the studio bureaucracy and submit it to his wife, chauffeur, mistress, agent, or talented nephew for further "improvement."

And what comes out will still bear your name.

In England, almost everyone—directors, actors, and writers—comes up from the theater. And you don't rewrite Shakespeare, Shaw, or John Osborne. You try to understand what they were getting at, the way an orchestra tries to interpret a symphony instead of rewriting it. And writers (rightly) own the copyright to their imagined compositions.

I have argued points with directors and producers in England until I wanted to kill—but it was always a one-on-one debate about something we both cared about. In America you deal with underlings who have their own personal agenda that contains little commitment to any one project, and certainly none to any writer, or his creative efforts.

For anyone who really wants to "write," it is a demeaning and soulless way to work—however rewarding financially. I know that if I had returned to America when I initially planned to, and somehow got involved with films, I would have soon got out. It is all too demoralizing. The wonder is that good films ever get made at all. Quite a few do, but when that does happen you can be sure it can be traced to one strong creative person big enough to defy the system. It may be a star, it may be a director, it may even be a producer, but it is never the writer. A good script is something everyone wants, but having given up their copyright, no writer has the power to do anything more than plead, cajole, and/or schmooze to protect the artistic honesty of his or her work. And if you argue too much, they will simply replace you, hiring someone else to work on your material, which they own.

On top of this, your self-esteem and pride—part of the spur at least—are knocked constantly, not only by the subordinate "employee" role you must play, but also by the fact that ideas and themes that are solely yours will inevitably be credited to someone else, usually the director. Only when it is a disaster—often *caused* by the director or producer—will the writer get his full "credit."

Currently it is possible—with a lot of luck—to direct your own scripts. Given the number of people trying to do this, the odds against it happening are enormous, and even those who succeed spend most of their lives wheeling and dealing, begging favors, and NOT writing.

And beyond that, many good writers are not natural directors, or even care to give their lives to so much detail and time-consuming drudgery.

Films are collaborative compositions: a good one needs wonderful direction, wonderful acting, imaginative technicians—and boy how they need a wonderful script. As you can tell by now, I do not believe the system is geared to getting them. One of the reasons we get so much violence, so much crude emotion, is that almost any executive can respond to that. Real emotion, real drama is something else again. Not so cheap. More difficult to achieve. More difficult to recognize.

But writers are not the lowest of the low in Hollywood (the aspiring starlet "who was so dumb she screwed the writer") because people don't want good scripts. It's because they are, unlike all their other professional colleagues, utterly powerless. Powerless to protect their material, powerless even to really argue its merits.

I don't imagine writers can ever get their copyright power back. Too much money, too many vested interests in the huge machine now to ever relinquish it. It is sad because I'm sure there are a few Shaws and Osbornes, Williams and Millers out there who could enrich and deepen the medium—and our times—by their vision and insights, but without the sword of copyright will never be able to do so. The medium will remain, in this country anyway, an "entertainment." I have nothing against entertainment, but civilizations grow and are remembered by their art.

And in a truly functioning film world one would not exclude the other. A few great films have already shown us what might have been.

Having said all that, however, I must confess to a life that has taken me to every corner of the world, has introduced me (literally) to princes and prostitutes, artists and murderers. I have learned so much each time I have taken on a new subject, I have met so many impressive and splendid human beings—some of them even in the industry!—that I know I have been blessed by the profession I stumbled into. I have been hugely lucky—especially in that some of the best work I have done was brought to fruition by some of the best work of greatly talented people. I am grateful for all that, and, for my life anyway, it has been a wonderful ride.

PATRICK S. DUNCAN

SCREENPLAYS

Beachgirls (1982) w/Phil Groves

84 Charlie Mopic (1989)

A Home of Our Own (1993)

The Pornographer (1994)

Nick of Time (1995)

Mr. Holland's Opus (1995)

Courage Under Fire (1996)

I was on a Writers Guild panel when another writer described how painful it was for her to write. She went into some detail about the great, wrenching labor and psychological horrors she went through, putting words on paper. And apparently she was not alone in this masochistic antipathy toward her craft. I've heard from and met many other writers who voiced the same tales of misery.

I have never understood the pain of creation.

I love writing. It is the best job I have ever had. And I've had some bad jobs. At one time in my life I drove a honey dipper. That is the truck you call in to vacuum out your septic tank when it overflows. I have hauled cinder blocks by hand, picked every fruit and vegetable grown in this United States. I have been an accountant, shoeshine boy, pizza cook, factory worker, soldier, and I swept floors and cleaned out the grease traps at a Kresge's.

Writing is a great job.

I don't break a sweat. There is no nine-to-five schedule. I get no blisters, no sunburn, or strange rashes from the fiberglass I've been sanding, or the insecticide they've been spraying on the fields while we're picking.

I don't have to wear steel-toe boots that guillotine your toes when you drop a heavy chunk of steel on your feet.

And there is no one shooting at me.

All in all, writing is a good job.

Sure, there is some downside. The usual volume of scut work that you find inherent in any job. There are the agents, lawyers, development executives, studio people, directors, and actors—but I have learned that there is an asshole quotient in every field.

I guess what the disgruntled writers are complaining about is not the business of writing, but the act of writing itself.

That is my favorite part.

I wrote before I was paid for it. I still write on spec, and I don't care if it sells or not. I write because I enjoy the process of writing. Because it is fun.

Every time I put pen to tablet I create a new world, a world that I control. I create characters to populate that world, characters that I love, and I give them problems over which to triumph (or not). It is a form of puzzle construction where I have the power to create my own solution. Again and again, I take human experience at its worst or best and explore, reveal to myself and, I hope, the reader.

I make movies in my head.

These films are cast perfectly, the actors utter my dialogue line for line, exactly as I wrote it. The sets and wardrobe are as I visualized. The special effects, God couldn't do better if he had Spielberg's money.

Of course, if the screenplay is produced, the result is never what I pictured in my mind. How could it be? That part of the process is frustrating. It always will be and I don't fret over it—at least not for long.

And I can return to that perfect movie in mind for a visit.

I love my characters so much that the last ten pages of a screenplay are always the most difficult to write. I don't want to leave them or their world. When I finally do write "The End" and leave, I have a sort of postpartum depression that lasts until I start a new story. So I start one, immediately.

I suppose I am a storyteller.

Maybe those complaining writers find the process so painful because they are writing for the wrong reasons. I know writers to whom this applies. They want to be rich, famous, get laid. They really want to direct, go to premieres, be part of a certain crowd, and so on.

But they don't really want to write. Writing has become the chore they have to complete in order to pursue the other things. So they hate writing.

I don't understand them. I spent the first thirty years of my life trying to find a job that I loved, the kind of job where I would get up in the morning and *want* to go to work. I would think I had wasted my life if I spent most of my hours doing something I hated.

But most people do and I imagine that is where a lot of the grief and suffering in the world is created.

Another aspect of writing, one over which I have no control but do appreciate, is the power we writers have as purveyors of popular culture. The day after *84 Charlie Mopic*, a Vietnam War film I wrote and directed, premiered at the Sundance Film Festival I met a man. Actually, he approached me and pointed to a woman standing across the room. "That is my wife," he said. "She was a nurse in Vietnam. We've been married for seventeen years and she has never talked about her experiences there. Last night we saw your movie and we stayed up all night while she told me what happened to her. Thanks." Many other veterans have since spoken of the impact the film had on them.

And *Mr. Holland's Opus* had a far-reaching influence. I have dozens of newspaper articles about "Mr. Ramidez' Opus" or "Mrs. Klein's Opus"—where some community has recognized and thanked some dedicated teacher. Scores of people have written to the former teacher who changed their lives to acknowledge that fact. School music programs have been reinstated as the movie proved to be a catalyst for parents and teachers to reverse such cutbacks.

Not bad for a former migrant worker.

This is a great job.

On a more personal level, I find an additional benefit to my craft that I never expected. Every time I write, I find myself going through a form of self-examination that is almost a kind of therapy. By creating and examining my characters I find myself questioning my own motivations, my own character. By creating problems for these characters, I look at my problems—and sometimes find solutions. If I get angry at something, the way teachers are treated in this country, the low opinion of women in combat (despite a few thousand years of history stating otherwise), I write about it and get *Mr. Holland's Opus* or *Courage Under Fire*. Trying to come to terms with my own combat experience, I delved into those subjects in *Courage . . ., 84 Charlie Mopic* and *War Story: Vietnam*.

Every story and every character has a part of me, good guy or bad, and I share their emotions, good or bad. I vent rage, weep, laugh, and all without exposing anyone else to my angst and dramatics. I take my worst psychological problems and work them out on paper. I think writers, like other artists, go into dark corners where most people have hidden the dangerous parts of their lives. Writers go into these closets in their minds, pull out something most people don't want to discuss or admit, and say, "Look at this. This is how I feel, how I think." And the wonder of it all is that no matter how despicable, dreadful, or embar-rassing that thought or deed may be, it is often universal. The audience recognizes it and experiences that same emotion vicariously, safely.

So I submit myself to this therapy—and sometimes get paid for it. I get paid to play in a toy box limited only by imagination. I influence the world in a small way, and I am immortal—at least my work will live much longer than I.

Can you think of a better job?

I can't.

JAMES V. HART

SCREENPLAYS

Gimme an F (1985)

Hook (1991), w/Malia Scotch Marmo

Bram Stoker's Dracula (1992)

Muppet Treasure Island (1996), w/Jerry Juhl and Kirk Thatcher

Contact (1997) w/Michael Goldenberg

SCREENWRITERS' 24-HOUR SUICIDE LINE

I wanted to do everything but be a Writer. Writing was not a real job. Those guys that got shot off horses or that did high falls off the castle—that was a real job. That and being the President or Errol Flynn. It never occurred to me that none of these jobs were real unless somebody faced a blank page and wrote:

"EXT. SHERWOOD FOREST - DAY"—before any or all of the above could result in a paycheck and a vocation in the movies.

However, in my thirties, when out of desperation, I finally started writing, it did not surprise anybody. People I had not seen in years would say, "Oh, you're finally writing, that's great, it's about time." It just took me a long time to figure out I had something to say.

From the time I was a kid I was fascinated by pirates. After my brother and I saw *Spartacus*, we went home and chopped down my mother's garden with our wooden swords. When I was in the sixth grade, I started reading Robert Heinlein and have been hooked ever since. Every Saturday morning there was a twenty-five-cent double bill at the

Gateway Theater in Ft. Worth, Texas, where I grew up. (You got it right, twenty-five cents, that is why I look like Gabby Hayes in my portrait.)

It did not matter how bad the movies were, every one I saw was "the best movie I'd ever seen." My friends and I went every week, then we went home and re-enacted the movie. My favorite death scene is James Whitmore in *Them*. It ranks up there with Robert Shaw in *Jaws* and still gives me the creeps.

But it wasn't until my wife and I had kids that I got back to my original love for fantasy in my writing. My children made me a kid again. I realized I had been buying toys before we had children. Fantasy was my way into writing.

The secret, the great key to writing *Hook*, came from my son. When he was six, he asked the question, "What if Peter Pan grew up?" I had been trying to find a new way into the famous "boy who wouldn't grow up" tale, and our son gave me the key. Our daughter, then three, ended up writing some of the best lines in *Hook* at age nine.

So I listen to my kids. Even now, at ages eighteen and sixteen, our story meetings continue, and both have become distinguished writers and directors of theater in their respective schools.

As for me, screenwriting has become a way of life. Every time I sit down to write, I am there because I am compelled to be. The little voice inside, the muse, the brain, the ideas, simply will not leave me alone until I write them down. You need that voice. You need to be compelled to write. It is not a casual vocation.

Screenwriting is the most difficult form of writing there is because there are so many rules, and eighty-seven people (who are not screen-writers) are waiting to give you their opinion. So, my advice: be driven to screenwrite. Do not be dragged kicking and screaming. Walk through walls, leap tall buildings, eat broken glass and baby ducks if that is what it takes to get those characters to leave you alone for an hour's rest.

I always remind myself that the screenplay is the currency that opens the door in this fantastic chaotic business. The screenplay, regardless of what you may hear, is everything. No story, no character(s), guess what, no movie. Hey, there are plenty of examples of "no movie" even with script and character.

Every time I sit down to write, or walk and think, I remind myself that I, me, the Screenwriter, am the asset, the gas, the juice, the verdi gris, that makes this big engine run.

Writers write screenplays. Not creative executives, Not lawyers, Not ad-pub departments, Not movie stars, and sometimes not even directors. They all can try and write screenplays, and many become gifted Screen-writers, but writing is the Writer's calling and task and duty in this business.

From Steven Spielberg I learned to collaborate, to let go of my personal vision of "my" story and learn to be a part of the team of incredibly talented people all working toward the same end. *Hook* was a great gift that I shall always be grateful for.

From Francis Ford Coppola, I learned that the job of the screenwriter is not to impose his or her own vision of the film on the director, but to help them achieve their own and hope on occasion the two are one and the same. *Bram Stoker's Dracula* taught me respect for the director, who is the writer first. Francis understands how hard it is to get those words on the page in the first place. Francis's lesson to me is, to be a great and complete Film Director one has to write, and be good at the craft and understand storytelling.

Storytelling is everything. Without the story, you can forget the interactive CD Cyberscanwavenetwebsite.

No story. No characters. No nothing.

Write screenplays until they line the sidewalks of New York and Beverly Hills. Write screenplays until people are wiping their hands and other places with them in the rest room. Write screenplays until they appear on the backs of producers' eyelids when they blink. Eventually, maybe even on your first try, some lucky person will be smart enough to read what you have leaped tall buildings, eaten broken glass, and stepped on baby ducks to write.

Continued Happy Thoughts.

James V. Hart

NYC, March 26, 1998

MICHAEL TOLKIN

SCREENPLAYS

Gleaming the Cube (1989)

The Rapture (1991)

Deep Cover (1992), w/Henry Bean

The Player (1992)

The Burning Season, cable telefeature *(*1994), w/Ron Hutchinson
  and William Mastrosimone

Deep Impact (1998), w/Bruce Joel Ruben

NOVELS

Flare (1988)

Among the Dead (1993)

PUBLISHED SCREENPLAYS

The Player, The Rapture, The New Age: Three Screenplays (1995)

My father was born in Russia in 1913 and moved to Canada in 1926 and then to New York in 1946 and got his first job in television in 1949 or so and then I was born soon after and then we moved to Los Angeles where I stayed until 1968 when I went east to college and lived for ten years and then returned to California in 1978 to write for the movies. My mother was a lawyer for Paramount.

I still love the idea of the movies, but these days I lie when I say I liked something. Most of the time I don't like what I see, or I like it a little, or parts, but not the whole, not with love. This frustration enters my work, I am sure. What can be done?

Ken Turan of the *Los Angeles Times* hated *Titanic* for its bad script, but he misses the point of screenwriting, which is to explore the anecdote for the camera. Blocks of dumb stuff put together properly can make a good movie. The novel cannot afford whatever is meant by bad writing, but neither can it afford intentionally clever writing unless that kind of writing is to your taste.

In the last few days I have watched the Powell/Pressburger *Life and Death of Colonel Blimp*, on laser, and then, also on laserdisc, the first forty minutes of Visconti's *Death In Venice*. Each is great. The movies are a lost art form, although there's still hope.

I read somewhere that in the generation after the golden age of Greek tragedy there was a version of *Electra* in which she saved her children. So it isn't fair to blame the movies for the debasement of culture. These are cycles. The current cycle includes the death of posterity, but this too shall pass. God resuscitates the dead and even posterity will rise again.

DALE
LAUNER

SCREENPLAYS

Ruthless People (1986)

Dirty Rotten Scoundrels (1988), w/Paul Henning and Stanley Shapiro

My Cousin Vinny (1992)

Love Potion No. 9 (1992)

They say it's impolite to discuss religion or politics at dinner. I don't think it's impolite, I think it's impossible. Because a discussion on this level usually involves an attempt to change someone's belief system—which is the impossible part. Even if they're wrong, especially if they're wrong—they will resist you at any cost. You can make the strongest argument imaginable and they'll simply disagree. You can support your argument with irrefutable facts derived from highly reliable sources, and it will be dismissed in favor of a supporting anecdote, or hearsay, or something they just made up on the spot. I had a friend who made up his own "studies." No matter what evidence you may provide, people by and large will remain unconvinced and unchanged. That's because belief systems are more often than not based in faith, and faith by definition does not include facts, logic or scientific methodology. It's a way of life, a commitment of sorts, and to change one's commitment to that belief would be tantamount to making them become disloyal, or worse—as if you were trying to change their very soul. And if you try, some people will bristle with resentment. Ever try to tell a little kid there's no Santa Claus? They *resent* you for it. You wanna piss someone off? Prove to them they're wrong. People don't like being *proved* wrong because that's like being proved they're stupid. Relentlessly corner someone intellectually, then prove to them they're wrong and ram home the truth? Oh yeah, they're gonna really hate you.

A kinder, softer approach is an annoying tactic parents often employ, the "Wait till you get older, then you'll understand" approach. That's really a variation on the "*I used to believe . . ."* approach, which is the "*I used to believe* the way you believe, but I have learned over the years that I was wrong and I have changed. And I'm wiser now." This is a good argument if used calmly, and if the subject respects you, and if your explanation as to *how* you came to change your belief system makes sense.

Which brings us to the *auteur theory. I used to believe in the auteur theory.* I don't anymore. If you don't know what the auteur theory is, then let me explain in a nutshell. A handful of French film critics in the '50s discovered that a handful of notable American films were directed by a handful of directors. They saw such consistency in these films that they would consider the directors to be the *authors* of those films. *Auteur* is French for *author*—hence the *auteur theory*. Were these directors the *authors* of their film? If you believe in the *auteur theory*, then directors are the authors of the films they've directed.

Somehow it's pretty commonly accepted that directors are somehow the authors of the films they direct—and not because of any compelling argument, but because it's so ingrained in our culture. For instance, I just looked at a copy of last month's *Entertainment* magazine, an issue dedicated to all movies coming out this year. Each segment tells us who's starring in the film and who directed it and also gives a brief story synopsis—but no mention of the writer.

Why is that? Is the director of a movie deemed *more important* than the writer? Now I pick up the *Video Movie Guide* for 1997, with "more than 17,000 movies on video!," 17,000 story synopses, 17,000 directors, more than 50,000 stars, *but not one mention of a writer!* Clearly, writers are taking a backseat. Ever seen a screenwriter interviewed on a talk show? Nope. And you don't see them on magazine covers. Everywhere you look, you see . . . well . . . no screenwriters! A movie star can burp in the middle of the night and it makes the papers. A screenwriter would have to kill a man and eat him to get press.

Yes, *I used to believe* . . .

When I was a film student, I was a devotee in the church of the director. I remember reading books with titles like *The Director as Superstar.* I pretended to be a Godard fan, since all the texts at the time seemed to revere him highly (though I'd never really seen a Godard film). I was honestly a huge fan of Kubric. and Hitchcock. My first student film was to be a highly cinematic and stylish thriller! Having taken every screenwriting class Cal State University at Northridge had to offer (two classes in all), I sat down and wrote a script.

Here's the story: a teenager is babysitting when she hears a weird sound coming from someplace inside the house—she investigates. As she walks through the very large home, the sound grows louder, and she eventually finds that it's coming from a closet in the back of the house. Tension builds as she reaches out to open the closet door—but she stops! She leaves the room. Goes back into the kitchen and gets herself a big carving knife. She returns to the room with the noise, goes up to the door. Her hand trembling, she grabs the doorknob, turns the handle, and *the door flies open*! And there's nothing there—just black—as though she were looking into another dimension! And then, and then . . . her hair blows up behind her—there's a huge sucking force coming from the closet, *it's sucking her into the closet*! She resists, falls, and grabs the floor, but it's useless she can't get a grip—and she is pulled into the closet! The door closes! And that's it. The end.

Alright, I'm not proud of that story—in fact it's pretty damn embarrassing seeing it in print, but I'm trying to make a point. I shot the film all by myself. In color. 16mm.

I wanted my friend Brad to look at the film. Brad was a young man with a bright future who'd won photography awards and wanted to be a director too. We were film buddies, we'd gone to the movies many times together and had long discussions over the merits of this film over that one. I respected Brad's taste as being as intractably snobby as my own. Brad came down to the school, and we went into the editing room, threaded up my film, and turned on the Moviola. And Brad watched.

Well, as the girl was wandering through the house, Brad was truly impressed, commenting very favorably on how great it looked, the lighting, the composition, the angles, the camera movement—the whole look was great. He was very impressed and told me so—and he was really involved in the film—asking me, "What's in the closet?" I couldn't have written a more enthusiastic response—totally involved—right up to the end, but not including the end. I was Kubrick and Hitchcock put together and I was only twenty-one! Then the end came—the door flies open, revealing nothing but darkness, and the girl gets sucked into the closet. Door closes. Story ends.

Brad was silent. I lost him, totally lost him. Whatever impression I had built up in the previous ten minutes was completely lost in the last thirty seconds. I was not betrayed by my directing skills, or my photography, or editing, or music, I was betrayed by my script, by my writing skills. No matter how well I directed a woman being sucked into a closet, it was still a woman being sucked into a closet.

Put Kubrick, Hitchcock, Huston, Capra, Scorcese, Wells, Spielberg and Coppola into a room and ask them to direct a woman being sucked into a closet. No matter how well or creative it is, you still have a woman being sucked into a closet. All the spices in the world can't make road kill taste good, and no matter how well you direct, shoot, stage, dress up, and score a woman being sucked into a closet, she's still being sucked into a closet! It doesn't make sense, no matter how it looks or sounds! The scenes before it set something up—a tension and a curiosity about what was behind the door—and no matter how you shoot the door, what kind of knife, the look on the babysitter's face—it's all irrelevant—the structure of the story, the *story itself* just didn't work. It was the writing that didn't work.

And when a movie works? It's the same way. The converse is true, that is, when a movie works, when a woman being sucked into a closet is a satisfying emotional payoff to the scenes that preceded it, when the audience *aches* for that woman to be sucked into the closet, when that woman's eternal dream has evaded her during her entire life and finally, in the end, her dream comes true and she is sucked into a closet. At that point the movie works.

Kubrick and his superstar director friends cannot screw up structure that works. But there are lesser directors who do some damage, some more than others, but ultimately a movie flies, floats, sinks, or crashes because of the script.

Well, I can't say I changed my beliefs right then and there, I'm much too stubborn to do that, but I did discover a newfound respect for writing that twenty years later still continues to grow. But I would learn that the more I directed, the more I could see that what works, works because it is somehow engineered to work in script.

After that experience, over the next six or seven years I honed my writing skills to a point where I actually sold a screenplay: *Ruthless People.* It was made and became a bona fide box-office hit, and it got pretty great reviews.

The reviews would often mention a scene or a moment or a situation that I'd written, and then proceed to give the director credit for it. Huh? It was at that point when I became a confirmed fallen Auteurist. What do they think a writer does on a film? What do they think the director is doing?

Then I'd meet people outside the movie biz who'd ask me what I do. I'd tell them I write movies, that I wrote *Ruthless People,* to which they'd usually respond, "That Danny DeVito, he's so *funny.*" Or "Bette Midler—she's *hilarious.*"

Later in the conversation, the outsider would *always* ask, "When you say you *wrote* the screenplay, just what exactly does that mean?" To which I would say, "I came up with the idea, wrote the entire story including creating all the characters, every scene, one scene after the other, what happens in the scenes, where they take place, what time of day, all the action, and everything all the characters said." And they would be silent for a brief second, and then they'd often respond with "Really?" They were *impressed and surprised.*

But some people were not, some would get quiet and *pretend* to be impressed. Pretend because they didn't really believe me. Oh yeah, they believed I had *something* to do with the story, that I probably came up with the idea and fleshed it out to a dozen pages or so, but that the actors wrote their own dialogue and the director said "Action" and later, after the actor improvised brilliantly, the director yells "Cut! Print!" I could see they didn't believe I actually wrote the entire screenplay, certainly not in the kind of detail I claimed. On top of that, some were politely resentful because (they felt) I was taking credit for something that Danny DeVito did, because they know for a fact that Danny made them laugh, that Danny *said* the words like they were his own! Don't get me wrong, Danny's a terrific actor, and like all terrific actors, he said the words *as though they were his own* because that's what terrific actors are expected to do. But they weren't his words, they were mine.

People may see a movie with a certain movie star, but only if the *story* sounds like a good vehicle for that star's charms. Put an action star in a romantic comedy and people stay away. Clearly people are heavily influenced by the story, and who writes it is (apparently) irrelevant.

So who does the movie belong to? In my opinion, as long as movies have stories, as long as they are based in fiction, they are filmed stories. The medium is film, but it's still fiction, it's still a story.

Take away the story and you have no movie.

LARRY KARASZEWSKI

SCREENPLAYS

Problem Child (1989), w/Scott Alexander

Problem Child 2 (1991), w/Scott Alexander

Ed Wood (1993), w/Scott Alexander

The People vs. Larry Flynt (1995), w/Scott Alexander

That Darn Cat (1997), w/Scott Alexander

I was born in 1961. Ten years later my parents were divorced. Not my fault, I swear.

My dad got custody of me for one night a week. He had absolutely no idea what to do with a kid. We would usually end up at a drive-in theater. This is where my love of movies began. Dad would bring a six-pack of beer and fall asleep while I watched the world's weirdest triple bills.

South Bend, Indiana's Moonlight Drive-In had an extremely eclectic booking policy. Where else could you see *The Sterile Cuckoo* and *Last House on the Left* on the same night? Exploitation crap from A.I.P. and Golden Harvest were presented on an unjudgmental, even playing field with *The Conversation* and *Amarcord*.

I ate it all up. I couldn't understand why Bruce Lee wasn't nominated for Best Actor. In my polluted eyes he was at least as good as Melvyn Douglas.

This crazy dichotomy has colored my entire professional life. It is why fringe characters like Ed Wood and Larry Flynt are incongruously given such high-class treatment. My very first conversation with Scott Alexander revolved around the films of Herschell Gordon Lewis. My career highlight was getting Milos Forman to sit through a casting session with Tom "Billy Jack" Laughlin. They loved each other.

I'm sure a psychiatrist would be aghast at introducing the works of Russ Meyer and George Romero to an eleven-year-old, but for me it's been the secret of my success. I'm positive I would now be a Hoosier factory worker if my parents had limited my viewing to Walt Disney. My kids are now ages two and four. When can I crack open that *Faster Pussycat! Kill! Kill!* laserdisc?

Maybe I'll start off slowly with *Cooley High*.

VELINA
HASU
HOUSTON

SCREENPLAYS AND TELEPLAYS

Journey Home, teleplay *Wonder Works* (1984)

Hishoku (1990)

Kalito, short (1991)

Summer Knowledge (1991)

Hothouse Flowers (1993)

Golden Opportunity, The Rest Test, Picture Perfect, True Colors, Leon for President, teleplays *The Puzzle Place* (1994)

PLAYS

The Legend of Bobbi Chicago (1986)

Broken English aka *The Melting Plot* (1988)

Tea (1989)

Snowing Fire (1993)

Japanese and Multicultural at the Turn-of-the-Century (1994)

Hula Heart (1995)

Cultivated Lives (1995)

Tell Her That You Saw Me (1996)

BOOKS

The Politics of Life: Four Plays by Asian American Women (1992)

The Matsuyama Mirror in *Short Plays for Young Actors* (1996)

Tea in *Plays for Actresses* (1997) and in *Unbroken Thread* (1993)

As Sometimes in a Dead Man's Face in *Asian American Drama: Nine Plays from the Multiethnic Landscape* (1997)

But Still, Like Air, I'll Rise: New Asian American Plays (1997)

Hula Heart in *Eight Plays for Children: The New Generation Project* (1998)

Kokoro in *Political Plays of the 1990s* (1998)

THE WRITING LIFE: HYBRID VIGOR
An Essay

Learning to Breathe

I began my literary life as a poet and now write in several genres—playwriting, screenwriting, television, cultural criticism-cultural studies, and, of course, poetry, to keep the soul alive. In addition, at the behest of my prose agent and with the insightful mentoring of a novelist whose work I greatly admire, I am writing my first novel, an adaptation of my signature play, *Tea*. I do not think of myself as any particular type of writer, but simply A Writer. That is what I told my mother I wanted to be when I began kindergarten in a strange, foreign country called the United States of America, which today is my home. Often, I have been tagged a cross-genre author. If I must be labeled in some way (and I know from personal experience how important labeling of individuals is in this country), I prefer that term because it represents the multiple-genre consciousnesses of who I am as an artist.

Many authors who specialize solely in one genre have criticized my enjoyment of writing in several, but my answer to that is simply that those who can, do.

Inspired by a native Japanese mother who encouraged me to write haiku and tanka at the age of five, and a drama teacher who said she found my poetry visually powerful, I wrote my first play as a pre-adolescent. Even then, I enjoyed exploring the multiple racial, ethnic, and cultural consciousnesses of my Amerasian history and reality. While my subject matter travels many roads beyond those today, they continue to inform me philosophically, which is an element of self that I feel is essential to the writer's psyche. The questions raised by philosophical examination and the enlightenment that can be wrought from such exploration is part of my process for fertilizing the raw materials out of which my writing grows. Long ago, I found myself embarking upon an extensive journey that would bring me from Japan to Kansas to California, during which my regimen for writing became as important as exercising the muscles of the body to maintain physical fitness. At an early age, I began to exercise the muscles of my mind, heart, spirit, imagination, and instinct—those writing muscles that so easily atrophy if not given constant attention. The regimen continues in force today complemented by vigilant philosophical inquiry and an artistic vision inextricably tied to the never-ending exploration and excavation of the human condition, with the hope that these peregrinations will not only ultimately entertain audiences, but also enlighten them—and me—to some degree or another.

Why I Breathe

I write because I must. The absolute necessity of writing was an early urge and remains so compelling in me that I prefer the pen over any other relationship—except the genuine and deep relationships that I have with my two children, Kiyoshi and Kuniko-Leilani. Like my relationship with my children, my relationship with the pen possesses a great deal of integrity, dimension, endurance, and honesty; and it is always there, challenging me to look beyond the horizon of what I think I already know, to attune and exploit my senses in ways that I never thought I could in order to discover more and more about humanity. Writer's block does not exist, except perhaps as a euphemism for those who are easily distracted, highly social, or simply resting. I certainly have never suffered from it from the day I first picked up a pen decades ago. If anything, there is too much to say, too much to finesse from raw ideas to the refinement of craft, so much that I know one lifetime is not long enough to complete it all. When I am not parenting, I am always writing. I am in the midst of one or another of the processes that carry the raw material to finished product. Perhaps even parenting sometimes is a part of that process because my children inform my life as a writer. They teach me more than books do and endlessly inspire me. They, more than any other human beings, have made my life meaningful and useful. I always have cottoned to Arthur Miller's declaration that a writer must live a useful life.

Instincts of Breathing

Writing cannot be forced. In deciding what to write and when any particular project should be pursued, I follow my instincts, unless, of course, I have a producer- or publisher-imposed deadline to meet. At those times, my energies in some way coalesce and focus upon a particular project in a powerful way that allows me to embrace that project and be absorbed by it so that nothing need be forced. Generally speaking, at times I am drawn to film, television, and theater projects; other times, to the novel and a book of cultural criticism that is in process.

My plays have been produced widely in Japan and the U.S., including productions by Olympia Dukakis and Jeff Daniels, as well as other theater productions from the Old Globe Theatre to the Smithsonian Institution. I have been commissioned by a host of theaters and institutions, including The Mark Taper Forum (two, one current), Manhattan Theatre Club, Asia Society, The Lila Wallace-Reader's Digest Foundation New Generation Play Project, The State of Hawaii State Foundation on Culture and the Arts, and others. In addition, my plays, along with my poetry and cultural criticism, have been published in anthologies and journals. Currently, an anthology of six to eight selected plays from my repertoire is being edited by Dr. Juli Thompson Burk.

In Japan, five documentary films have been produced that examine my work and my family, including films by Japan's leading producers such as NHK and Mainichi Hoso. My plays have been produced there with popular and critical embrace, and are taught at some of Japan's leading institutions of higher learning. Moreover, I have been invited to lecture at the Japan Foundation and other cultural institutions. The response has been welcoming and added greatly to the usefulness of my life experiences.

I have edited two anthologies of American plays written by persons of Asian ancestry, *The Politics of Life: Four Plays by Asian American Woman* and *But Still, Like Air, I'll Rise: New Asian American Plays*. I also have edited an anthology published by the University of California at Los Angeles of multiracial creative writings and intellectual discourse, both literary and visual, as a special edition of the *Amerasia Journal* entitled *No Passing Zone*, which brought together expressions of hapa and multiracial culture from around the globe.

As a screenwriter and television writer, I always have worked for hire, usually being hired on the basis of either my playwriting or earlier scripts written for hire. Until this year, I had never written a spec script. This is largely due to the fact that my plays originally served as samples of dramatic writing (and still do), and that, after the first job, my screenplays written for hire served as writing samples as well. While I have never set out to sell my plays to film, my current screenwriting assignment happens to be an outgrowth of my plays. Early in its life after an off-Broadway production and two California productions, my play *Kokoro* was optioned for film, and I was hired to adapt it to the screen. My other work, all work-for-hire, mostly is unproduced, but includes studio work, projects with indies, and both produced and unproduced PBS projects with *WonderWorks* and *The Puzzle Place*. Because, in the past, I never have exerted exorbitant or radical effort in my screenwriting career, but still managed to get hired, I feel fortunate, especially because, along the way, one of the things I did was to contribute to quality, educational television programming for children, which as a parent is vitally important to me. While finishing two playwriting commissions and having a second child, I did not work for hire as a screenwriter. In fact, over the course of my career, I have taken time off in my writing career to manage two difficult pregnancies and two unexpected major surgeries. Now I am writing my first genuine spec script because I want a new writing sample that speaks to my current artistic expression.

Along with this vigor, I decided to write a (non-fiction) book about multiracial identity and its representations in cinema and popular culture. The desire was an outgrowth of a long sociopolitical career of representing the postmodern multiracial community and my exhaustion over the fact that so many scholars seem bent on deconstructing my multiracial and multicultural hapa identity in their writings, and usually with a large degree of inaccuracy. The book became my dissertation after I decided to return to school and obtain a Ph.D. in critical studies in cinema and television. The program, the requirements for which I have met save the completion of my book, enriched my perspective of my fields of research. The book, *All Mixed Up with Nowhere to Go: Cinema and the Mythology of Multiracial Identity*, is scheduled for completion in 1999.

Concurrent with the development of the non-fiction book, I began an adaptation of my signature play, *Tea*, to the novel, seeking out a mentor who possessed a powerful, incisive, and yet lyric voice and who would be willing to help me get my arms around the new genre and its demands. I have spent two and a half years being mentored by T. Coraghessan Boyle (*The Road to Wellville*, *The Tortilla Curtain*, *Riven Rock*, and countless other books) as I struggled to embrace and fuse with the genre, only slowly to understand that, in being a writer of plays and screenplays—a writer versed in dramatic writing—I was already closer to the novel form than I had ever imagined. In returning to my dramatic instincts and revealing story scenically as well as focusing on the dramatic methodology of showing versus telling, I began to find my stride as a novelist, coupled, of course, with the power of the story I have to tell and the lyricism that, for better or worse, is innate to my artistic voice. I could not have even come this far without my agents' support and patience, my mother's encouragement and belief in me; and Boyle's constructive criticism, candidness, belief in my project, and encouragement. With care, I continue with the novel and make progress, especially considering the fact that this progress develops in tandem with the development of my non-fiction book, my three "post-pregnancy" new plays, the current film job, a new spec screenplay, two new television spec scripts, the rigorous management of my physical fitness, and the priority creative project of my life: the successful single-parenting of my children, both of whom are gifted with intellectual brilliance, poetic souls, and passionate hearts. I have had to jump a lot of hurdles in my life, but, if my children are the reward for the hardships I have faced, then I am glad to have faced them. Blessings, indeed.

Many ask how I manage to do so much. I do not know. I do know that I manage time well and I do not suffer fools very readily. It has been rumored that I have a clone. Some say I am an alien. I just know that the muses are never quiet and, what is more, never are any genres packed away for a respite. All the genres I mentioned above sit at my fingertips waiting for a respective journey to begin. I write prolifically and concurrently, my mind precise and powerful. Of that and my parenting I am utterly confident.

In the same way that I follow my instincts to determine what genre will be given my attention at any given time in my creative life, I listen to those instincts about what literature to read or what films, plays, or good television to view. I must confess my love for good literature and, again, I do not read simply in one genre, but across several. I can receive as much pleasure from reading a non-fiction book of cultural criticism about a sociopolitical issue or a philosophy book as I can from a fine novel or beautiful poetry (which has mystified some of my solely novel-reading literary colleagues). There is always a book in my life. That interest never flags and also never fails me. In the same vein, I feel that it is important as a writer for me to expose myself to the literature of film, television (good television only, please), and theater. To that end, I make it a point to see a variety of films and plays, and a bit of American, English, and Japanese television.

Sharing Air

Another part of my creative life that has been an interesting and often rewarding journey is my existence as a mentor to screenwriting and playwriting students, particularly the many highly motivated and brilliant students in the Advanced 434 Screenwriting Workshop in the

Department of Film and Television at the University of California at Los Angeles, my alma mater, where I have taught. Currently, I am on the full-time tenured faculty at the School of Theatre, University of Southern California, where I have the privilege of mentoring undergraduate and graduate playwriting students as a resident playwright and director of the playwriting program. Working with my screenwriting students over the years and trying to inspire them to greater heights and deeper excavations has been immensely satisfying. In addition, on the whole, they are a personable, ambitious lot who, rather than just commanding respect, give it back to others, including their mentors.

As an artist, I feel it is important to take what I have learned and feed my energies back into new writers, to encourage their creative vision and help them in their journeys from idea to script. Of course, I have been fortunate to mentor screenwriting students who represent some of the finest creative minds from around the world because the UCLA program attracts large numbers of applicants, and those who are admitted are the best of the best, but the chief attraction of teaching is to be able to give of my gift to others. Pointedly, screenwriters are not taught per se, but mentored. They can be taught craft, but they must bring their innate talents to the table. Their vision and the determination necessary to bring that vision to fruition must be extraordinary and driven by the utmost passion. The vigorous desire to make something happen—against the tremendous odds of the arts and entertainment industry—is mandatory for writers.

Mentoring new screenwriters can be a highly creative process and experience, especially when you have the right writers sitting around the table. For the most part, working with new writers has been a positive experience for me, and I remain committed to it as part of my creative life.

Complexities of Breathing

The discipline of creating dramatic structure in playwriting is much more challenging than the novel or screenplay. The more confined world of the play, for the most part, cannot call upon cinematic technique or the literary and kinetic flexibility and agility of prose to aid in the executing of a plot. Crafting of dialogue and character that allows the story to be shown rather than told, poetics, and dogged attention to dramatic structure are all one has to reveal story in theater. One has to be prodigiously and acutely creative and imaginative to do what needs to be done dramatically. That is why understanding how dramatic structure works in a play is good preparation for understanding how it must work in screenwriting or in the novel.

That, however, is not to suggest that abundant common ground exists across genres. Certainly, the novel, the play, and the screenplay all own a scenic reality and dramatic reality that have their parallels. How those realities are executed in terms of craft, however—complemented inseparably, of course, by a writer's own vision, style, and artistry—are distinct. I know that, depending on what kind of project is my focus at any given time, I have to switch gears in my mind. The switching of those gears, however, is a very facile adjustment for me. Being able to write, and especially to write across genres with ease, perhaps is aided by my prodigality of patience—enriched by my life as a mother—as well as life experiences that have left me no choice but to seize each and every moment and fill them with my compelling desire for creative expression.

The Art of Breathing

The way in which my muses speak to me and the ways in which I can apply their music to (multiple) craft are my pot of gold at the end of the rainbow. Life has delivered to me its shares of blows that have often left behind some spiritual detritus from which it took years to recover, but I heal and forge ahead with determination and mettle, encouraged by the positive offset of the gifts I have been given—my children and my art. Because of them and the love and support that my mother, Setsuko, has been kind and generous enough to give to me in spades, life is rich.

To quote the late poet Delmore Schwartz: "God is in love, in love with possibility." Anything is possible. And sometimes what appears initially to be impossible becomes possible with patience and perseverance—and poetry.

Every day, there must be poetry.

The End

March 20, 1998

ANGELO PIZZO

SCREENPLAYS

Hoosiers (1986)
Rudy (1993)

I've never considered myself a "real" writer; the term that feels more comfortable to me is filmmaker. What I do is make a movie in my head, then translate it to the page. Words are the necessary tool to communicate the movie I've imagined but, unlike novelists or journalists, I see the words not as the end but the beginning. (No screenwriter aspires to have their work published, only produced.) The screenplay is by far the most important part of the transformation of idea to finished film, but it should be remembered that it is still a part. My role as the producer of the movies I've written has been, in some critical ways, like hiring of cast and crew, as important as the words I put on paper.

I never dreamed or desired to be a writer . . . of any kind. My first five years in the film business I worked as a producer and production executive. Like many, if not most, in that position, I often allowed myself the conceit that I could have handled this or that scene, or sequence, better than the writer with whom I was working. When the company employing me disbanded and paid off my contract, I was put in the position to test that conceit. Having taken screenwriting classes and read close to a thousand screenplays, I thought I was prepared. I wasn't. I foundered badly, losing confidence and then stumbling through a year of dead ends and hundreds of pages of unusable scenes until, finally, a version of *Hoosiers* emerged. After many drafts and four years of rejection, the movie was finally made and ended up doing pretty well . . . ever since, people have defined me as a writer.

Many assumed that reading those thousand or so screenplays was a helpful training tool. But if I learned anything, it was in the order of what *not* to do. The problem was that ninety-eight percent of those screenplays were mediocre to poor. The two percent that were special were always of a singularity of vision, and that vision was not mine.

Why were most those screenplays and (movies for that matter) so bad? A few thoughts . . .

1. Screenwriting classes. Most deconstruct and analyze successful films to discover their key paradigms or formulas, suggesting that screenplays are nothing but great big Rubik's cubes, whose "secrets" once revealed can be reconstituted with your idea to create a masterpiece. Ah, if it were only so easy. This "outside in" approach invariably produces screenplays with an often logical structure but an inorganic hollow core.

2. The Great Lottery . . . prospective writers wanting to strike it rich by selling their spec script for millions. If this is the starting point,

then the "outside in" problems are made even worse. These writers desperately aim to please by trying to figure out what is selling. The imitative approach almost always misses what separates good scripts from the bad and the ugly . . . originality and vision.

3. Lack of Narrative. The biggest single technical downfall was the inability of the writers to tell compelling stories. I read many screenplays with great characters and individual scenes or sequences, but the narrative drive, rhythm, and pace was rarely there.

From the negative to the positive . . . A few ideas important to me.

Before writing Fade In:

A. I should be able to verbally tell the story I'm about to write in two-minute, five-minute, ten-minute versions. My primary goal is to get an audience swept along in the story. I read the listeners' face and body language . . . if they don't *really* want to know what happens next, I find another story.

B. I need to know generally where I'm going with my story, but give myself the room for discovery along the way (but am always specifically clear about my destination—the end).

C. I make sure to identify the central idea or theme of the piece and think of it as the aortic vein—that from which all flows.

D. I cannot write a story that doesn't have a personal emotional resonance and a locus where the screen story and my own story meet.

E. I aspire for a balance between the universal and the unique—the most successful films exist on familiar landscapes (genres) but make you feel like you've never been there before.

F. Movies are short for moving pictures . . . I try to tell the story with character behavior and action. If I wanted to dramatize a story through dialogue, I would write a play.

G. Once started, I never look back—the ever-present rewrite critic perched on my shoulder is the biggest obstacle in getting to those magic words Fade Out.

H. The ratio of the time I talk or read about writing to the time I actually write is about 1:1000.

MARK ROSENTHAL

SCREENPLAYS

The Jewel of the Nile (1985), w/Larry Konner

Superman IV: The Quest for Peace (1987), w/Larry Konner

The In Crowd (1988), w/Larry Konner

Desperate Hours (1990), w/Larry Konner and Joseph Hayes

Star Trek VI: The Undiscovered Country (1991), w/Larry Konner and
   Leonard Nimoy

For Love or Money (1993), w/Larry Konner

The Beverly Hillbillies (1993), w/Larry Konner

Mighty Joe Young (1998), w/Larry Konner

Mercury Rising (1998), w/Larry Konner

Screenwriters are twice crazy.

Once crazy like every other writer. Solitary confinement by choice. Each day alone in a room, wrestling thoughts into words, forcing them into some kind of order, at times like coaxing a swarm of hornets back into the hive using one bare hand.

Twice crazy because, after months of writing, when other writers complete their work and send it on its way—screenwriters begin a second greater task: pulling everything apart again at the suggestion of a committee composed of producers, studio executives, actors, development executives, assistant producers, cameramen, spouses, caterers—anyone and everyone. All because no one assumes that the opinions of the person who actually created the story and the characters have any more weight than anyone else's opinions. As if they all had an equal hand in creating it. And with an absolute lack of self-consciousness, they will dismiss the writer's ideas, or more usually the writer himself or herself, because they honestly believe he or she had nothing to do with the story. It simply belongs to everyone. It's a kind of psycho-airbrushing.

Stalin's dark room had nothing on Hollywood. When I hear someone say California is a community-property state, I always assume they're talking about directors and writers, not husbands and wives.

We once had to listen to an assistant junior development executive defend her notes on a script we wrote about Washington, D.C., by saying, "I know this world. I almost minored in political science at USC."

We wrote our first screenplay in the food court of the newly opened Beverly Center mall. Mostly because it had cheap food, rest rooms, and lots of stores to waste time in. I had found the idea for the script in the back of the *New York Times*—a small note about a young girl, a teenage thief, in India who was eluding police, hiding out in sympathetic villages. We turned her into a strong-willed, heroic girl from Florida and in two weeks finished her odyssey in screenplay form. I was back home in Philadelphia waiting for my father to come out of the ICU after triple-bypass surgery when my partner called and told me we'd sold this first screenplay in two days. The euphoria lasted until the night I returned to L.A., when the phone rang. It was the director who'd just been put on the project calling to say, "I can't make any movie I haven't written myself, so you're fired." We ended up having to sneak in line with a group of teenage girls to see a screening of our film. It took me four months to recover from what they had done to the story. Since that time I never see any movie made from one of my scripts.

I follow a Red Adair approach to Hollywood these days. I fly in on a few days notice, check into a hotel, fill forty-eight hours with non-stop meetings, cap the hole, and get out covered in grease. Living back east in the civilian world is actually a great aid to screenwriting. Real people with real lives and real problems. In Los Angeles everything is seen through a scrim of ambition and anxiety. It's a DeChirico distortion and dangerously distracting to a writer.

The joy of screenwriting comes from its pure narrative requirements. It's a little like haiku in its need for compression (prose is an expansive art form, by contrast), like comic books in the tumbling, out-of-control gait that forms the rhythm for each beat, and, most of all, like storytelling as it first must have developed along with language—a secret shared that seeks to elicit "Tell me what happened next!"

Never take a film course. Don't you dare waste your family's hard-won money on film school. There's nothing you need to learn there. Being born in the United States means you "speak" movies fluently—it's our universal slang. We explain our lives to ourselves within the illusion of movies. We play an internal soundtrack behind everything we do. Just listen to little kids at a playground and you'll hear them punctuate their play with film-score flourishes. In America, everyone has two professions: their own and show business.

ED
SOLOMON

SCREENPLAYS

Bill & Ted's Excellent Adventure (1989) w/Chris Matheson

Bill & Ted's Bogus Journey (1991) w/Chris Matheson

Leaving Norman (1992)

Men in Black (1997)

TELEVISION

It's Garry Shandling's Show

HARVESTING RAGE AND SELF-DOUBT FOR FUN AND PROFIT OR WHY I WRITE

There's a joke about a screenwriter who is having trouble completing a script. Finally, on the night before it's complete and with less than half of it written, he breaks down in front of his computer and, sobbing, he does something he never thought he would do: he prays to God for help. After a good deal of wailing and pleading, the ceiling parts and a booming voice comes down from the heavens and literally *dictates* the rest of the screenplay. And it's brilliant. The writer is overwhelmed with gratitude and emotion and, offering himself as a humble servant to his new Lord, he begs God to let him know how he can ever repay Him. God listens, ponders this a moment, and then respectfully tells the screenwriter that He thinks, perhaps, He would like to share writing credit. The screenwriter then slowly raises his head, peers through the gaping chasm in his roof, and tells God to go fuck Himself.

At some point we all lost the sense of why we were doing this writing thing. We started, somehow, with ideas and ideals, and now most of us are driving nice cars and are living in nice homes and are constantly comparing the sizes of our decks. Okay, I'm lying. We didn't all start with ideas or ideals. I sure didn't. I started because I didn't believe I had any *actual* talent. Writing, to me—at least in seventh grade—seemed like a way to make myself stand out a bit. So while my friends were sitting on floors playing "House at Pooh Corner" on their guitars, I was straining to crack jokes or flailing around with a pen and a notebook writing *extremely* lame "comedies." My earlier titles were things like *Cleveland Five-0* (an absolutely inept *Hawaii Five-0* "parody"), *The Monster That Ate Cleveland* (apparently I thought that things were funnier if you set them in Cleveland), and *M*U*S*H*M*E*L*L*, one in a series of (so-called) comedies starring a repellently unfunny detective named Marvin Mushmell. I still have them—I think there are seven thirty- or forty-page books in all—and I look at them every few years just to remind myself that whatever writing abilities I may have are not, in fact, God-given. If anything, all early signs point to a struggling twelve-year-old just trying to make sense of his demons and screaming to be heard. Cut to:

Now. And the same holds true. Except I am thirty-seven.

JOAN
TEWKESBURY

SCREENPLAYS AND TELEPLAYS

Thieves Like Us (1974), w/Robert Altman and Calder Willingham

Nashville (1976)

Old Boyfriends (1979), directed only

Tenth Month, telefeature (1979), directed

Acorn People, telefeature (1980), directed

Canary Sedan, teleplay *Alfred Hitchcock Presents* (1983), directed

Elysian Fields, network pilot (1988), produced and directed

Cold Sassy Tree, cable telefeature (1989), directed

Sudie and Simpson, cable telefeature (1990), directed only

P.I.N.S., teleplay *Shannon's Deal* (1980), directed

Wild Texas Wind, telefeature (1991), directed only

Windows, teleplay *The Stranger* (1992), directed

On Promised Land, cable telefeature (1994), directed only

Scattering Dad, telefeature (1998), directed

PLAYS

Cowboy Jack Street (1978), directed

Jammed (1997), directed, produced

Dance Card (1998), directed, choreographed w/James Canfield

PUBLISHED SCREENPLAYS

Nashville Screenplay (1977)

WRITING TO SEE IN THE DARK

Writing pictures is weird. Interesting, challenging, involving, but wrong. Movies are to watch, to feel, to be involved with, but not to read.

Writing for film is like diving from a moving airplane into the ocean without a parachute and while falling through the water being instructed to prepare a gourmet meal in half an hour with unfamiliar ingredients that everyone has to love.

Sometimes it's fun, sometimes it's hard. Sometimes it's trips to exotic locations. Sometimes it's lucrative, sometimes it's not, but it's always mysterious, and ultimately the challenge of walking to the desk to greet the blank page or screen is a daunting task.

A hundred "how to write a screenplay" books have been written, but there is no formula for fortune and, contrary to popular belief, not every outing grosses a million dollars. Writing movies is not math or brain surgery, but it is complex in structure and complicated by the number of people who are paid to have an opinion about your outcome. I find the best defense against these conflicts of collaboration is laughter and a gambler's dedication to "the action." Hard work satisfies my ongoing addiction to the work ethic, but the love of process, the gathering of obscure details, and the sense of discovery satisfies a curiosity that originates in the soul.

At the beginning, anything I write is usually boring. Flat, dull, clogged, cluttered, a quagmire of mediocre metaphors that limit the possibility of anything new to appear. Sometimes there will be a real rush, like a power surge, letting you glimpse the project's potential, but often it will disappear as quickly as it came.

In an effort to shock my system I'll deliberately deprive it of everything except coffee. That only lasts a few days because I can't stand the vacuum, so willingly I rush to do research, but "information," like one square of chocolate, is never enough, and becomes a respectable excuse for not writing. Getting lost in the thicket of history, swept away by behavior, current events, last night's dream . . . after all, one thing leads to another. Each trail meanders to a path, and every path is a game of chance. Will it be a dead end, a landslide, the peak of the heap, which doesn't even get into the business of serendipity.

Because your focus is on Vienna or cigars or spies or Eleanor Roosevelt or "Tootsie" Queeler from East L.A., life begins to present you with coincidental overlaps, glimpses, chance meetings . . . an old boyfriend who just got back from Vienna, a friend of Eleanor's granddaughter, a woman who rolled cigars in Cuba, a parade of low-rider cars from East L.A. You're possessed, convinced that you are hearing pertinent conversations in passing, be it restaurants, airports, or hotel lobbies. You're so busy gathering you forget to pay the phone bill, you forget to eat, you forget you've just eaten, you win the lottery, you lose the ticket, your mother dies.

Scraps of stuff swirl around like bad radio signals from China, Milan, Albany, Siam. Swimming in overlapping sounds, a cacophony of possibilities. Out of desperation you plug in Bach, hoping it will underscore, focus the noise, give a gentle push toward organization, but it doesn't work. It's not time yet.

Next you clean out your closets, pay the bills, wax the floors, shop for a sick friend, offer to take the second grade to the planetarium, offer to take the dog to the vet, and make a dental appointment. Still nothing happens.

Now you get mad. Outrage at the Republicans, the Democrats, the rich, the poor, the famous, the invisible . . . shouting at the television set, the newscasters, sports fans, talk-show hosts, contestants, the dog, the cat, the kids . . . Finally everyone leaves you alone so you can indulge a brief interlude of self-pity, self-doubt, and loathing. Convinced there is nothing left in your talent pool, you make the decision to become a cleaning lady or a salesgirl at Saks. Then, suddenly without warning, the world, the world of your very own creation, rolls over, begins to spin differently on its axis.

An image, one image blasts its way up to the conscious surface, bypassing the barricaded brain. One image, black and white, color, it doesn't matter. One image is all it takes to walk to the desk, but until it arrives, often while sitting in the bathtub, I cannot begin.

One hundred white turkeys gobbling down a red-dirt road in rural Georgia . . . crisp green money being stuffed into the bright red g-string of a thrusting male pelvis, slamming against a room full of screaming women . . . a shiny black pickup truck, hovering mid-air against a blue Texas sky, being lowered by screeching crane into a huge hole cut out of a tiny church courtyard in Odessa, Texas. Its owner inside, sitting upright and dead. Grinning from ear to ear under his hat . . .

Suddenly like the great floods in history, the dam breaks and there's no stopping the flow. Right or wrong, it cascades, it pours, you can't get the words down fast enough. All those scraps, all those crossed radio signals, the music, the jokes, the books you read, the people you overheard, the people you talked to in cyberspace or interviewed along life's blue highways. Finally it gels, it clicks, and you cancel everything: the trip to the vet, the dentist, taking the second grade to the planetarium.

You stop shopping, cleaning, moping. You are a frenzy of focus, a facilitator of fine ideas, a trafficker of tricks with the wisdom of Moses, Christ, Buddha, Freud, and Bucky Fuller coursing through your veins. You are the Bill Moyers of questions and answers, the Nostradamus of dark, the Robin Williams of light, the Cole Porter of clever. You are happier, healthier, thinner, smarter, more prolific, more generous, more spontaneous, more gifted, and more unreliable than anyone your family or friends has ever known. But . . . you are, at last and once again, a writer.

One page or two, five or fifteen . . . it's a miracle. One word after the other, black lines on white paper, neat, orderly. It is always a surprise, a constant source of wonder, totally unexpected and welcomed with awestruck humility.

Why do I write? I have no choice. If I don't write, I disappear, I shut down. The whole bunch of me ceases to manage myself. Pen to yellow paper, words in longhand, often misspelled, these are my keys on the piano. It's the only way I can carry a tune, on key or off, fast or slow, Beatles or Bach . . . It's how I know I'm here.